CHANGING FACE OF POVERTY AND GLOBALISATION

G.P. ISSER

GYAN PUBLISHING HOUSE
NEW DELHI-110 002

Changing Face of Poverty and Globalisation
(Social and Economic Development)

Rs. 590

ISBN : 81-212-0791-6

Published in 2002 in India by
Gyan Publishing House
5, Ansari Road, New Delhi-110002
Phones : 3261060, 3282060, Fax : (011) 3285914
E-Mail : gyanbook@del2.vsnl.net.in
Website: http:\\www.gyanbooks.com

Lasertypesetting by : Varsha Graphics, Delhi
Printed at : Chawla Offset Press, Delhi

For

Godavari, Rajesh and Poonam

Contents

Preface

The prevalence of widespread poverty in the developing world has aroused the conscience of mankind. The statistics can hardly capture the deprivations that the poverty inflicts upon those who are affected by it. Poverty has to be felt through the wet eyes of the poor who have to make hard choice between nutrition and shelter, between medicines and education. As a result of lack of "capabilities", they survive without meeting the basic needs of their life. While elimination of poverty is urgent and is a deeply human objective, study of the subject misses the focus because it gets shrouded by a haze of controversies. My main objective in this book is to clear this haze and to delink the study of poverty from the ideological overtones that the debate on poverty often evokes.

Towards this end, it is imperative to separate the analysis of poverty from the study of distribution of income which suffer from ideological bias. More often, reducing poverty is associated with reducing inequality and is perceived to influence distribution of income in the society. I would like to make it very clear that reducing inequality and reducing poverty is not the same objective. The concern with poverty is to improve the living conditions of that segment of society which is below the line of poverty and is most deprived in terms of basic needs and facilities for living. To lift them up from the line of poverty, through targeted anti-poverty policies, will not influence differences in the standard of living in the higher income categories. In other words when our objective is to ameliorate the conditions of poor, we are not distributing the resources for achieving equality of income. There have been perceptions that for the alleviation of poverty, re-distributive measures have to be undertaken and that would result in slowing the momentum of growth. The book aims at clearing this kind of "mix-ups" in ongoing debates through analytical and empirical research. In the study of poverty, one of the horizons that emerges is that poverty alleviation is not necessarily conditioned by re-distributive policy. It is the pattern of growth which determines the choice of policy for reduction in poverty and not necessarily the policy of redistribution that is viewed to affect efficiency and productivity adversely. The endeavour to bring out this clarity in the perception on poverty, will to a great extent help in shaping the policy framework for alleviation of poverty without allowing it to be diluted in the streams of controversies which are not relevant for the study of poverty.

Another important thought which is developed in the book is to bring out the links between economic growth and reduction in poverty through empirical research. Through case-studies of development experience, the study brings to focus the significance of reducing poverty for sustainable economic growth. When we remove poverty, we meet an objective that is humanitarian and also we strengthen the foundations for higher rate of economic growth, which is, sustained in the long run.

In an era of globalisation the choice of policy is necessarily and increasingly influenced by external environment. My objective in this book is to study the interaction between the forces of globalisation and the elimination of poverty from the developing world. As we all know that globalisation has gainers and losers. The study points out to the various policy initiatives at national and global level to enable the poor participate in the benefits of globalisation. The United Nations millennium summit 2000 has adopted declaration on the eradication of poverty within time-bound framework. This reflects growing global consensus on fighting poverty and brightens the prospect for international cooperation in meeting this development-goal.

And finally for me, the study of poverty has been almost natural. I have seen poverty in and around villages where I spent my childhood and revisited it again in various parts of the developing world during my diplomatic assignments. I always thought to provide some inputs through academic work towards the shaping-up of policies to combat poverty. The present book has grown out of the study and research which I made towards meeting this goal.

G.P. Isser

Acknowledgements

The analysis in this book centers around two basic themes viz., poverty and globalisation. With fast changing development—scenario and especially with speeding globalisation, it was not possible to capture the changing economic parameters without the cooperation and assistance given to me by several organizations and institutes. I drew on the collection of materials and information in various libraries and documentation centers. In this regard, I must acknowledge with grateful thanks the help and assistance rendered to me by Director, (library) Ministry of External Affairs, Librarian, National Council of Applied Economic Research (NCAER), Librarian, Research and Information System for the non-aligned and other developing countries (RIS), Librarian, World Bank Documentation Center, Librarian, United Nations Information Center (UNIC). and Librarian, United Nations Development Programme (UNDP). They extended excellent cooperation to me in my present work.

To understand the multi-faceted dimension of poverty in its totality, an endeavour in this book has been made to project the poverty-profile of the "poorest of the poor" in the developing world. Writing on these aspects, required a mass of uptodate material, and statistics related to the dynamics of development of the "The Least Developed Countries", LDCs. This was facilitated by the study of the LDC Reports of UNCTAD which incorporate very comprehensive analysis of development scenario of LDCs. The analysis of special problems faced by the Least Developed Countries in combating poverty in Chapter-III is primarily based on LDC report of 1999 and 2000. I owe special debt of gratitude to the Secretary General of UNCTAD for this. I also take this opportunity to express my grateful thanks to Professor G.K. Galbraith, a former diplomat and distinguished Economist for according his permission to quote from his book "The Nature of Mass Poverty".

In facilitating my task of collecting statistics related to poverty profiles of developing countries, the functionaries of World Bank, UNIC, UNDP gave valuable support. I extend my grateful thanks to them.

In process of completing the book, Shri B.P. Garg, Managing Director, Gyan Publishing House made valuable suggestions. I owe words of gratitude to him. I had commendable help from Shri Amit Garg, Director (Production) Gyan Publishing House in organising various aspects of publication such as design etc. Shri Pritam Giri from editorial staff provided much needed assistance in completing the book. I extend my grateful thanks to Shri Amit Garg and to his colleagues.

Introduction

The persistence of mass poverty in an era of massive technological capacity to create wealth presents major challenges for the economists and for the policy-planners. In past, the economists responded to the challenge of times and through their theoretical and conceptual innovations, made important break-through in the understanding of the crisis that the time presented. In classical era the quest for mankind was how to create wealth. Adam Smith through his Book, "Wealth of Nations," enlightened the mankind on the ways and means to produce and create wealth. Later, after 1870s the neo-classical economists through their conceptual innovations guided the mankind how to determine the reward of factors of production. In 1930s, the mankind faced a major crisis of prolonged depression and unemployment and Keynes in his book "General Theory" prescribed the cure for this. The problem of poverty has however continued to haunt the mankind from generation to generation and even today in 21st century, the existence of poverty and deprivation presents major challenge to the progress that mankind has made during last two hundred years. While on the one hand there is an unprecedented affluence for some people, more than a billion people live in abject poverty in developing world. This book starts with the response of economists that they made to this problem from time to time. In chapter I, the book brings together responses of leading economists from classical to post-war era who gave divergent perceptions on this phenomena. Chapter I examines the perspectives on poverty which have undergone very rapid and fundamental changes. The rethinking on development that has taken place in the post-war development economics, has added new dimensions to the analysis, study and research on the various aspects of poverty.

The new dimensions "inter-alia" include concept of lack of capabilities, which measure the degree of deprivations suffered by the poor people. According to current thinking on the subject, poverty is no longer perceived only in terms of low income but it has become a multi-dimensional phenomena. The new definition of poverty is in terms of human deprivations such as lack of safe drinking water, lack of sanitation, lack of education etc. The task for the eradication of poverty assumes urgency and also becomes more challenging in terms of the choice of policy. This is the message that the analysis of chapter I conveys to the readers.

The development experience of four decades has opened new contours for the study and analysis of poverty across the globe. Some countries succeeded in making spectacular gains in converging towards developed countries and were able to reduce incidence of poverty very substantially. Chapter II puts together the experience of successful developing countries especially in East Asia who were able to nearly wipe-out poverty from their countries. The empirical evidence collected from the case-study of these countries shows a very close relationship between the rate of economic growth and the decline in poverty. Republic of Korea achieved tenfold rise in per capita income between 1965 and 1995 and was able to reduce poverty to negligible level during a very short span of time. Similarly Thailand, Malaysia, Indonesia made considerable gains in their per capita income in 1970s and 1980s and succeeded in bringing down the level of poverty significantly.

The case-studies in Chapter II, analyse various policy-initiatives that were undertaken by the countries in the East Asia which resulted in decline in poverty. The study brings to light that it was not only the high rate of economic growth that contributed to reduction in poverty but it was the pattern of growth which was of crucial importance in making the impact of economic growth on poverty. Chapter II through its analysis of development strategies adopted by Republic of Korea, Malaysia, and Indonesia etc. also brings out the impact of development policies on the fulfillment of basic needs of the population. It brings to focus the package of social and human development policies, which was instrumental in eliminating the human-poverty in terms of deprivations suffered by the people. The study in this chapter also shows how the development of human resources which was crucial to the rapid economic growth of the East Asian countries led to the removal of poverty. It is through these policies that appropriate social conditions were created along with the process of economic growth that resulted in the decline both in income and human poverty.

Chapter III brings out the most daunting challenge for the developing countries in eradicating poverty. There are a number of countries in the developing world who have been trapped in the low income – equilibrium level and where economic growth has been either negative or negligible. Chapter III identifies the bottlenecks faced by these countries categorised by the United Nations as the Least Developed Countries (LDCs). The Chapter focuses on the persistence of poverty and deprivation that have inflicted sufferings on the 600 million people living in 49 countries falling under LDCs group, mostly in Africa. The study of the growth – pattern of these countries shows that for these "poorest of the poor countries", the elimination of poverty calls for special efforts and policy initiative at both National and International level. The study of the dimension of poverty also leads to the conclusion that unless the poverty is removed from these countries, the international development goal of halving poverty by 2015 cannot be attained.

Indian experience in poverty-alleviation provides useful inputs for the study of poverty in the developing world. Poverty in India can be adequately analysed in terms of diverse experience that the constituent states of India has got in their fight against poverty. A comparative survey of the success of various states in lifting the poor people above the line of poverty has been attempted in this chapter. The study brings to light the importance of the choice of policy for the eradication of poverty. The analysis also covers the status of social and human development in various states and brings to focus the success of Kerala in fulfillment of basic needs such as health care, education, sanitation, etc. The past performance of India as a whole in bringing down the incidence of poverty has varied from time to time. The emerging trend reflects a close relationship between economic growth and reduction in poverty. In view of large number of people still below the poverty line, the analysis in this chapter identifies creation of employment-opportunities as the number one priority for the policy makers.

Indian performance in the fulfillment of basic needs also forms the part of this chapter. The analysis in this chapter scans through the lens of social indicators in the various areas of social and human development such as life expectancy, malnutrition, child-mortality, illiteracy, access to safe drinking water, access to sanitation etc. The survey of the various social indicators points out to the need for increase in investment in the social sector so that an effective dent is made in human deprivations and impoverishments.

Globalisation is now a dominant feature of world economy. It is manifested by rapid growth of international trade, capital flows, increasing importance of services in international trade, increasing global integration etc. It has led to revolution in information technology which has generated new foundations for development. Inspite of these positive outcomes of globalisation in terms of increasing trade, foreign investment and expanding worldwide income, the gains and losses of globalisation have been widely debated. Chapter V brings out this debate in the context of the prospects for the eradication of poverty from the developing world. For some developing countries who integrated with the global economy in course of their economic development, globalisation has contributed towards higher income and poverty-reduction. The study in this chapter brings out positive features of globalisation which have helped in the eradication of poverty and which also brightens prospect for developing countries in bringing down the incidence of poverty.

Towards the close, the book examines the new developments in the global economy and how these can be related to the eradication of poverty in the developing world. The new foundations of development have changed the traditional factors of production. Land, labour and capital have become less important when compared with technology which has expanded production-frontiers. Until recently capital was a scarce commodity but with globalised market and with growing integration, the access to capital has widened. Today it is knowledge that has become the prime mover of economic growth. In the new environment it is the human resource which is of vital importance. It is through the development of human resource that progress in future can be sustained. These changes in the global economy, give added importance to the elimination of poverty in the developing world so that the human resources in these countries are fully developed and utilized for growth and development in the global economy. The creation of wealth today is knowledge based and the revolution in information technology has added new dimensions to the need for human development. What is needed is to counter those trends which create technology and digital divide in the world because unless we are able to bridge these divides, it may not be possible to realise optimum gains from globalisation.

CHAPTER I

Emerging Perspectives on Poverty : Response of Economists

In classical economics, poverty was considered to be a natural state of humanity. According to the law of diminishing returns and according to Malthusian theory of population, a long run stationary state was predicted. In Malthusian theoretical framework, majority of people suffered from poverty because subsistence always lacked behind the growth of population.

Thomas Malthus explained the inevitability of poverty in following words:- "Famine seems to be the last, the most dreadful resource of nature. The power of population is so superior to the power of the earth to produce subsistence for man, that premature death must in some shape or other visit the human race. The vices of mankind are active and able ministers of depopulation. They are the precursors in the great army of destruction; and they often finish the dreadful work themselves. But should they fail in this war of extermination, sickly seasons, epidemics, pestilence and plague, advance in terrific array, and sweep off their thousands and ten thousands, Should success be still incomplete, gigantic, inevitable famine stalks in the rear, and with one mighty blow, levels the population with the food of the world".[1]

In Malthusian thought any scheme of equality was unsustainable on the ground of inexorable population problem. In his view, population control was necessary for the solution of the problem of poverty. In classical economic thought, especially in Ricardian and Malthusian scheme, poverty reflected the limitations of human productive powers and as such it was held as indispensable phenomena. It was with the advent of industrial revolution that it was realised that poverty was an optional state rather than a reflection of limitation of human productive powers. The two foundations of the classical perception of poverty as an inevitable result of law of diminishing returns and lack of subsistence resulting from increasing population floundered on the rock of evidence.

In the neoclassical economic thought, poverty was not considered as a natural state of humanity, which was the corner-stone of classical economic thought. In neoclassical thought it was marginal productivity of a factor of production which determined its value and hence the differences in the income of various factors of production resulted from the marginal return of the factors of production. In neoclassical perception, differences in income-level of factors of production resulted from their marginal productivity. Since low income of a person resulted from relatively lower marginal productivity, poverty did not emerge as an issue for a separate analysis in economics within the theoretical framework of the neoclassical. In neoclassical thought, the emphasis had shifted to the determination of the value of individual factors of production according to their marginal productivity. It was micro economics that dominated the economic thinking of the neoclassical economists and it was yet another contributing factor to keep the analysis of poverty out of the mainstream of economic analysis.

While the neoclassical economics concentrated on the micro analysis of economic variables, new dimensions of economics also emerged during this period. Economics was oriented towards the study of welfare of mankind. The neoclassical economists such as A.C. Pigou and Alfred Marshall brought to focus the need for economists to study the ways and means to increase the welfare of mankind. The slowly evolving shift in economic analysis towards the study of welfare of mankind was reflected in the 'Economics of Welfare' written by A.C. Pigou, the Pioneer of Welfare Economics. The prevalence of poverty influenced Alfred Marshall's thoughts. J.M. Keynes recalled his views on poverty and inequality in a quotation from one of Marshall's lectures which is reproduced below :[2]

"From Metaphysics I went to Ethics, and thought that the justification of the existing condition of society was not easy. A friend, who had read great deal of what are now called the Moral Sciences, constantly said: 'Ah! If you understood Political Economy you would no say that'. So I read Mill's Political

Economy you would not say that.' So I read Mill's Political Economy and got much excited about it. I had doubts as to the propriety of inequalities of opportunity, rather than of material comfort. Then, in my vacations I visited the poorest quarters of several cities and walked through one street after another, looking at the faces of the poorest people Next, I resolved to make as thorough a study as I could of Political Economy'.

Through the words expressed above, Marshall linked the study of poverty with political economy. The study of economics was earlier subjected to severe criticism by philosophers such as Thomas Carlyle who called economics as a dismal science on the ground that it dealt with materialistic pursuits. Marshall gave a new orientation to the study of economics when he defined economics as a study of mankind. In his thoughts as expressed above one can see early insights into the modern concept of "Human Face to Development".

While some economists supported welfare orientation to the study of economics, it was not till the birth of development economics in 1950s , that perspectives on poverty starting taking shape in clear terms. Classical theory of economic growth was main thread in economic analysis till post-war era when economists started thinking in terms of development theories as a separate sub-discipline of economics.

In classical scheme of thought, capital accumulation was key to the creation of wealth. The classical economists such as Adam smith, David Ricardo, Thomas Malthus, J. S. Mill, they all made accumulation of capital, the main catalyst of economic growth. It was the maximization of savings which was generated from inequality of income that was crucial for economic growth in the theoretical frame-work of classical economics. The neoclassical economics also supported the link between capital accumulation and economic growth. In this scheme of thinking, to generate savings sufficient for capital accumulation, inequality of income was held to be an indispensable condition. Since high level of savings is a pre-requisite for rapid growth, income must be concentrated in the hands of rich who could save and invest.

Later, Keynesian theory of capital accumulation also supported the high-income-savings-investment nexus. In his famous book "Economic Consequences of Peace (1919), Keynes related the inequality of the distribution of wealth with the accumulation of capital under capitalism. He expounded his concept of relationship between inequality and economic growth in following words:

"Europe was so organized socially and economically as to secure the maximum accumulation of capital. While there was some continuous improvement in the daily conditions of life of the masses of population, society was so framed as to throw a great part of the increased income into the control of the class least likely to consume it. The new rich of the nineteenth century were not brought up to large expenditures, and preferred the power which investment gave them to the pleasures of immediate consumption. In fact, it was precisely the inequality of the distribution of wealth, which made possible those vast accumulations of fixed wealth and of capital improvements, which distinguished that age from all others. Herein lay, in fact, the main justification of the capitalist system. If the rich had spent their new wealth on their own enjoyments, the world would long ago have found such a regime intolerable, But like bees they saved and accumulated, not less to the advantage of the whole community because they themselves held narrower ends in view".

While Keynesian economics introduced changes in the basic postulates of classical and neoclassical economics, it did not discard classical nexus between saving – capital accumulation – investment. Once again income – inequality was perceived to be a necessary condition for economic growth.

The 1950s presented a watershed in the evolution of economic thought. The global economic scenario reflected growing income gaps between poor south and rich north. The poor and the rich divide between nations and within nations shifted attention of the economists towards the investigation of the causes of poverty in underdeveloped countries. The growing pockets of poverty in Asia, Africa and Latin America surfaced in the post-war era. The global economy presented a scenario of contrast which could not be explained within the classical and neoclassical framework of self-equilibrating mechanism which was operated by invisible hand. These developments, on the one hand brought the problems of underdevelopment within the theoretical frame work of economics and on the other hand brought the focus on the phenomena of mass poverty in the developing world.

While the development economists in the post-war era analysed the causes and cure of underdevelopment, they debated the link between inequality of income and economic growth. Some development economists such as W.A. Lewis (1954), a pioneer of development economics, supported the link between economic growth and inequality. Lewis argued that given the unlimited supply of labour in a developing economy, growth results in higher profits than in higher wages and hence inequality will continue as a trend. At a later stage when surplus labour is exhausted and wages begin to rise, the benefits are widely distributed.[3] Another economist Simom Kuznets in 1955, expounded the thesis that in the early stage of economic growth, inequality will increase and in the later stages it will decrease. In his classic paper, based on long-run time-series data for three developed countries (the USA, England and Germany), Kuznets hypothesized a time path of inequality for nations undergoing economic development with an increase in inequality in the early stages followed by a decrease in the later stages. This has come to be known as the Kuznets U-shaped curve hypothesis on the relationships between inequality and development.[4] Later, Kuznet's hypothesis on the co-relation between inequality of income and economic growth was not found valid on empirical evidence. It was found out that the relationship between inequality and economic growth depended on the pattern of economic growth followed by the developing countries and empirically it was not possible to establish that inequality was a necessary condition for economic growth in the developing world. East Asian development experience clearly demonstrated that along with growth, poverty was also reduced. It was established through empirical evidence that the policies which produced broad-based growth also led to decrease in the inequality of income and reduction in poverty. In the Newly Industrializing Economies (NIEs) of East Asia, for example, as firms expanded output, they also expanded their demand for labour and that resulted in raising the level of income of the poor. Economic growth of labour-intensive character benefited the poor and that invalidated the hypothesis of Kuznets that there was a necessary link between inequality of income and economic growth. The cross-country studies undertaken by economists such as Michael, Bruno, Martin, Ravillion and

Lyn square, also could not lend support to Kuznets hypothesis. The economists discarded the pessimism that economic growth is necessarily associated with rising inequality. It was widely held that the relationship between economic growth and reduction in poverty was a variable relationship which depended on the pattern of economic growth. This transformation in development thinking led to the perspective that there was no trade-off between economic growth and reduction in poverty.[5]

The analysis of poverty as an important aspect of development thought and of development policies got further momentum in the writings of development economists such as Gunnar Myrdal and T.W.Schultz. Through their analysis they found out a positive co-relation between equal distribution of income and economic development. Myrdal's view on the equality of income represented path-breaking concept in growth-economics. In his Essay he wrote "the productivity of higher consumption levels stands for me as a major motivation for the direction of development policy in underdeveloped countries. Higher consumption levels are a condition for a more rapid and stable growth".[6] The co-relation between equality of income and economic growth which was focused by Myrdal was in sharp contrast to the conventional thinking on the relationship between income inequality and economic growth.

Key contribution of Myrdal to the analysis of poverty was to dispel the belief that there was a conflict between the goal of economic equality and growth. He argued that inequality of income will not result in savings in underdeveloped countries because in these countries there was a tendency to squander income on consumption and investment. He also stressed that malnutrition and lack of elementary health and educational facilities bring down the productivity of poor people and therefore by raising their income, their productivity will increase in the early stage of economic development. Myrdal's thoughts, thus significantly contributed towards bringing the problem of poverty eradication to the center-stage of development agenda of developing countries.[7]

The theoretical foundations for the analysis of poverty as a part of the main-stream of development economics further built up when some of the development economists questioned the primacy of capital accumulation for economic growth. The economists recognized that growth was not only a function of capital accumulation but also of investment in human capital. It was in the writings of Schultz that the contribution of human capital to economic growth was brought to focus. If human capital was important for economic growth, the growth itself suffered when poverty prevailed in a society because the poor people are not included in the productive process of a developing economy. The emphasis on capital accumulation as the chief contributory factor in economic growth was debated after it was recognized that human capital is an important factor of production for development.

Economics of poverty came in to its real shape after the publication of the book entitled "The Economics of Being Poor" by Schultz. Schultz expressed his thought on poverty in the following words "most of the people in the world are poor, so if we know the economics of being poor, we would know, much more the economics that really matter" He had also noted that there is no integrated body of economic knowledge and no agenda of economic hypothesis to get important economic question about poverty. Schultz believed that economists can address the problem of poverty and expressing the optimism he said "poor people in low income countries are not prisoners of an iron–clad poverty equilibrium that economy is unable to break".[8]

In the post-war era of development thinking, the growing concern of economists on poverty was also reflected from the writings of J.K. Galbraith who brought to focus the issue of poverty in his book. "The Nature of Mass Poverty 1979". He added new dimensions to the analysis of cause and cure of poverty in his book under reference. He wrote "Poverty is man's most powerful and massive affliction. It is the progenitor of much further pain from hunger and disease on to civil conflict. The first is to combat accommodation. It is by universal education, literacy and its employment that individuals gain access to the world outside the culture of poverty and its controlling equilibrium. The second is to facilitate that escape. Economic development consists in enlarging the opportunity to escape the equilibrium of poverty and culture".

In Galbraith's writings one finds some of turning points in perspectives on poverty. His emphasis on universal education as a means to escape from the equilibrium of poverty has become one of the main determinants of policy choice for the eradication of poverty in 1990s. The other aspect that Galbraith emphasized in his writings was economic development as a means to escape the equilibrium of poverty by enlarging the opportunities for the poor.

While theoretical base for the analysis of poverty was slowly evolving, Dr. Amartya Sen's writings on development added new dimensions to the analysis of poverty. His writings which included poverty and Famines (1993), An Essay on Entitlement and Deprivation (1981), commodities and capabilities (1985), gave new insights into understanding poverty and contributed significantly to bring it to the focus of development thinking in post-war era.

In Dr. Sen's view 'Poverty is not just a matter of being relatively poorer than others but of not having some basic opportunities of material well being what he termed as the failure to have certain minimum "capabilities". The capabilities are of different kinds, i.e., being free from starvation, from hunger, from under-nourishment, from participating in community life etc. According to Dr. Sen, poverty is not a matter of only income but is is failure to achieve certain minimum capabilities. Sen's thoughts also brought to light deficiencies of conventional theories to apply income approach to the development analysis. Dr. Sen's capability based approach to poverty contrasted with seeing poverty only in terms of low income. Poverty cannot be analysed only in terms of income deprivation but more appropriate approach will be to see whether a person has ability to pursue well being. Income deprivation is only one aspect of poverty. It is not high or low income, but whether the income is adequate enough to generate minimally acceptable capabilities. Dr. Sen clarified that to have inadequate income is not a matter of having income level below an externally fixed poverty line, but to have an income below what is adequate for granting the specified levels of capabilities for the person in question. In his thought Dr. Sen emphasized that a person must have basic capabilities to obtain the elementary physical necessities such as nourishment, clothing, shelter, etc. Because of capability failure, a poor person is deprived of amenities and facilities such as health, services, education, etc. Even though there may be sufficient income, a poor person may be deprived of these basic needs and services and so social and educational conditions become important to determine the degree of poverty in a society.

Dr. Sen's focus on poverty as the lack of certain basic capabilities such as ability to avoid hunger and illiteracy not only revolutionized the development thinking in the post-war era but also enlarged the scope of policy framework for the elimination of poverty. According to Dr. Sen, in an economic system, a set of entitlement relations evolve. These relations are determined by ownership of the assets and by exchange entitlements. In other words, an individual's entitlement depends on the physical and human capital assets that he owns. That gives him ability to acquire the alternative bundles of commodities through production or thorough trade. Dr. Sen's analysis made eradication of poverty amenable to policies which influence the ownership of assets and which affect exchange entitlements. Several policy options for elimination of poverty emerged from these relationships. Poverty can be eliminated if we can make employment opportunities available for the poor. It can be also eliminated by the direct provision of basic needs such as primary education, basic health care, housing, sanitation, and safe drinking water.

The entitlement — approach to poverty, which was, conceptualized by Dr. Sen, represents a marked improvement on the approach that prevailed earlier. Kuznet's approach to income-inequality did not leave any option for policy choice in eradication of poverty. In his analysis, inequality of income was a trend inevitably associated with economic growth and as such, it has to be accepted by the policy makers. The advantage of entitlement approach to poverty is that it assigns a significant role to public policy in terms of its impact on poverty.

The shift to capabilities from income in understanding poverty had solid foundations in the diverse social outcomes of economic growth in developing countries. In early 1990s, a cross-country analysis of per capita income and social indicators of some developing countries showed that relatively few of the richer developing countries gave their people lower ability to survive with life expectancy varying between 53 and 66 years than some lower income countries who gave life expectancy of more than 70 years. This applied not only to life expectancy but also in case of education and health. The attainment of higher capabilities of poor people was not always the result of higher income, but of different public policy. This new policy perspective on poverty put emphasis on creating necessary conditions for removing mass deprivation in terms of basic needs rather than creating income alone.

The capability approach to the analysis of poverty in the developing world brought out the limits of income-centered concept of well being. In the new conceptual framework, the eradication of poverty did not depend only on increase in the income of the poor but on the build-up of requisite capabilities of the poor. In terms of policy it meant that poverty could be eliminated only when the basic needs of the poor could be fulfilled. This approach also led to focused attention on the pro-poor public policies for improving longevity, literacy, basic health, sanitation, which was ignored within income approach towards poverty alleviation.

The development experience of the three decades starting from 1950s also weakened the income approach to poverty eradication in the developing countries. When the development – era began in 1950s in the third world, it was expected that economic growth, in its process would distribute the benefits of growth in all the segments of the society and poverty will be eliminated. The empirical evidence of persistence of poverty in the developing world in 1970s and in 1980s showed that the so-called "trickle – down" effects of growth were not enough to make the powerful dent in the poverty. The publication of "re-distribution with growth" by Hollis Chenery and others in 1974, presented a serious attempt to re-orient the development strategy in the developing countries towards basic needs as a priority concern of policy makers.

The emphasis of economists on the role of consumption in economic growth provided foundations for the application of basic needs approach in development strategy. In new thinking, health and efficiency was basically linked with economic growth. The economists recognised that the greatest obstacle to ensure this linkage between economic growth and human development was the existence of mass poverty in the developing countries.

A consensus among economists built up that the intensity of poverty in a developing country could not be measured only in terms of income but it was necessary to assess poverty in terms of human deprivations.

The link between human deprivation and the intensity of poverty gave new thrust to empirical analysis of poverty – profile of developing countries. To assess human poverty and its degree, comparative social indicators such as life expectancy, access to health care, to safe drinking water, to education etc. were used to determine the degree of relative human poverty. This shift in the perspective on poverty led to rethinking on development strategy. It was soon recognised that while economic growth was a necessary condition for poverty eradication, human development can be achieved in varying degrees by the developing countries. The success in elimination of human poverty primarily depended on the pattern of economic growth and on the nature and content of public policy.

In the beginning of post-war development-decade which started in 1950s, it was assumed that when per capita GNP rises, it will result in a higher income for all. The distributive issue of development was to a great extent side-tracked because it was expected that the benefits of economic development would "trickle-down" to poor. The progress in data-collection and statistical analysis of income-growth and distribution in the developing countries showed that increase in GNP did not necessarily translate into reduction in poverty. While the development experience demonstrated that economic growth was not a sufficient condition of attacking poverty, the focus shifted to the identification of factors which caused poverty in the developing world. The question that the economist asked was how to identify the poor and how to measure the incidence of poverty. The search for a formula to measure poverty led to the drawing of national poverty lines. The lines were defined in terms of household income per capita, which would give minimum necessary consumption of food etc. Households with per capita income below the poverty line were defined as poor and those with income above that line were not catagorised as poor. Apart from national poverty lines, for analysis of poverty at cross-country level, it was necessary to have global poverty line. The World Bank determined the global poverty line of dollar 1 per capita per day to determine absolute poverty in the developing countries.

The national poverty lines provided useful data for the measurement of poverty in the developing countries. It was not possible however to measure the degree of deprivations suffered by the poor in terms of the lack of basic needs such as health, literacy, sanitation, housing, etc. By 1980s, in the conceptual evolution of poverty, the lack of human capabilities was recognized as a crucial factor. A person is poor not only because of his low income but also because he lacks access to health care, education, sanitation etc. In the 1980s, the analytical tools for poverty assessment were further improved and social indicators were applied to assess the comparative degree of deprivations of the poor in the developing countries which could reflect the lack of fulfillment of basic needs. In 1990s the United Nations Development Programme (UNDP) introduced several index such as Human Development Index (HDI), Human Poverty Index (HPI). Through these indices, the degree of impoverishment in terms of basic necessities of life and of capabilities was measured.

The improvement in the analytical tools enabled the national government and the international community, to assess the widespread poverty both in terms of income and in terms of human deprivations. The poverty profiles which were prepared by the UN agencies and by other organizations, led to a global consensus that the goal of economic growth could not be achieved unless the development was given human face. The world summit for Social Development which was held in 1995 in Copenhagen reflected this growing consensus on the need to eradicate poverty as a goal of economic development.

The social summit called on the participants to eradicate extreme poverty and to reduce it substantially within a time-bound framework. The time-bound targets, "inter-alia" included reducing adult illiteracy by half between 1990 and 2000, to raise average life expectancy to 60 years by 2000 etc. The resolutions of summit and the specific targets may be seen at Annexure I-1

The global consensus on the need to eliminate poverty within a time-bound frame-work led to fixing of targets in terms of specific programmes both at national and international level. The analysis of poverty in the developing countries was included in the development studies undertaken by International Monetary Fund (IMF), by the World Bank and by the United nations. The United Nations Millennium Declaration on 19th September 2000, incorporated targets for the eradication of poverty. The member countries resolved to halve, by the year 2015, the proportion of the world's people whose income is less than one dollar a day and the proportion of people who suffer from hunger and, by the same date, to halve the proportion of people who are unable to reach or to afford safe drinking water. The resolutions of summit related to the eradication of poverty in the developing world is at Annexure I-2.

Thus, the consensus on the enhancement of human capabilities as an index of economic development added new dimension to analysis of poverty. It was generally agreed that capability gives a person capacity to avoid ignorance disease, under-nutrition and early mortality. These capabilities cannot be created just by increasing income through the process of economic growth. To create these capabilities the application of basic needs approach to designing developmental strategy was essential.

The shift in thinking on poverty made the task of assessment of the level of poverty more challenging and complex for the economists and policy-makers. The UNDP developed a human poverty index which was a combination of the degree of achievement in meeting basic needs such as health, sanitation, water, housing, etc. These were measured by life expectancy, literacy etc. The empirical evidence of success in meeting the basic needs by some developing countries suggested that even with relatively lower income, developing countries could eradicate human poverty. Some of these countries such as the Republic of Korea, Malaysia, Sri Lanka, Mauritius, Costa-Rica, Cuba etc. achieved high degree of social development because they gave priority to education and health in their developmental strategy.

The emphasis on the eradication of human poverty through the fulfillment of basic needs in some of the developing countries showed noticeable link between the improvement in social indicators and the degree of economic growth. It was realised that high rate of economic growth was achieved by those countries who achieved high degree of social and human development. This invalidated the conventional wisdom that for economic development inequality of income and hence persistence of poverty was an unavoidable phenomena. It made Kuznet's thesis unacceptable and brought to focus a positive relation between reduction in poverty, development and economic growth.

Perspectives on poverty continue to change both in theoretical and policy aspects. The global consensus on the eradication of poverty from the developing world within set targets to be achieved in a time-bound frame-work represents a significant conceptual advance since classical era when it was accepted as an inevitable scourge of mankind. The beginning of 21st century has witnessed a number of policy initiative both at national and international level to eliminate this implication on mankind completely. At present stage of evolution, the perspectives on poverty differ mostly in terms of the choice of policy. There are several areas of conflict in policy terms which will need to be resolved if goal of the elimination of poverty is to be achieved. In determining the right combination of policy, economists and policy makers have debated various issues. These include the role of state in tackling poverty vs the role of market. The other issue around which the debates have centered is to determine the primacy of economic growth vs pattern of growth. The choice of strategy to eradicate poverty is complex and touches on various social and economic issues which are sensitive and are prone to conflict of interests among social and economic groups.

There has been a growing consensus that the development experience of countries who succeeded in reducing poverty, provides useful inputs for the determination of anti poverty policies to be adopted by the developing world. In this context, the nineties have witnessed abounding mass of studies which have documented the interaction between economic growth and alleviation of poverty in several countries. It is through this kind of empirical evidence that ongoing debates on alternative strategies can be resolved. The study of this evidence takes us to Chapter-II which presents case-study of selected countries.

References

1. Thomas Robert Malthus—An Essay on population-Everyman's—1914.
2. Quoted by J.M. Keynes in volume 1 of the collected writings of John Maynard Keynes : Macmillan and company – 1972, London.
3. Lewis W.A.(1954) Economic Development with unlimited supplies of labour, Manchester school of Economic and Social Studies – 22- 139-91. Lewis – W.A Theory of Economic growth – London, Allen unwin-1955.
4. Kuznets, Simon (1955), "Economic growth and income inequality- American economic review – 45, 1-28.
5. Since 1970s, the empirical evidence of success of some of the East Asian Countries in combining high rate of economic growth with alleviation of poverty generated fresh debates on the linkage between inequality of income and economic growth. For detailed studies following books and documents can be referred to :-
   - Adelman, Irma and Cynthia Taft Morris (1973), Economic Growth and Social Equity in Developing Countries, Stanford, CA: Stanford University Press.
   - Adelman, Irma and Sherman Robinson (1978), Income Distribution Policy in Developing Countries: A Case Study of Korea, Stanford, CA: Stanford University Press.
   - Anand, Sudhir and S.M.R. Kanbur (1993), 'Inequality and Development: A critique', Journal of Development Economics, 40, 42-50.
   - Deininger, Klaus and L. Squire (1996), 'Measuring Income Inequality : A New Data Base', World Bank Research Observer, 10, 565-91.
   - Article Entitled Equity and Growth in Developing countries "Old and New perspectives on the policies issues by Michael Bruno, Martin Ravallion, and Lyn squire published in the book income distribution and high quality growth (ed) Tanzi and Chu.
6. Gunnar Myrdal's Essay entitled "International inequality and foreign aid in retrospect", published in World Bank Publication "Pioneers in Development".
7. Gunnar Myrdal in his Book "The challenge of world poverty" – Allen Lane Penguin Press – 1970, gave important reasons why economic growth and economic equality should be combined in underdeveloped countries. In his view, conspicuous consumption of the rich reduces the investment from higher income of landowners etc. In the developing countries. The other reason advanced by Myrdal was that malnutrition and lack of elementary health reduces the productivity of the mass. Myrdal, there fore argued that equality is a condition of economic growth.
8. Theodore W.Schultz. "The Economics of Being Poor" – 1993 – Blackwell publishers Cambridge U.S.A.

CHAPTER II

Changing Face of Poverty : Case Studies

The developing world has been engaged in the task of eliminating poverty for last several decades or so. Since the world summit for Social Development (1995) was held in copenhagen, targets were fixed for reduction of poverty and the participants made commitments to reduce poverty within a time-bound framework. The United Nations Secretary General in its report entitled "Implementation of the first United Nations Decade for the Eradication of Poverty (1997-2006) reviewed the progress made by the developing countries in various regions in the eradication's of poverty.

The perusal of Secretary-General's report shows changing face of poverty in the developing world. There has been marked progress in reduction in both income-poverty and human poverty. The comparative performance of developing countries, region - wise at Annexure II-1 shows that the decline in the number of people in the developing world has been mainly due to reduction in the number of poor in East Asia. In South Asia, the share of people living in poverty declined but the total number of poor increased through 1990s. This was mainly because of increasing population in this region. In Sub-Saharan Africa even though the share of the population living in poverty declined, the number of poor people increased. In Latin America the share of the poor people in the total population remained constant but the absolute number of the poor people increased.

The changing region-wise poverty profile of the developing countries is at Annexure II-2. While there has been a significant reduction in global poverty, regional trends in the persistence of poverty in 1990s are alarming. As compared with 1987, the number of poor people increased from 474 million to 522 million in South Asia in 1998. In Sub-Saharan Africa the number of poor people increased from 217 million in 1987 to 291 million in 1998. In Latin America also, the number of people increased from 64 million 1987 to 78 million in 1998.

On the other end of the spectrum, the number of poor people in East Asia and pacific sharply declined from 415 million in 1987 to 278 million in 1998. The development experience of the successful countries in achieving significant reduction in poverty leads to new contours in the determination of development strategy to be adopted by the developing countries. The case-study of the successful countries such as Malaysia, Indonesia, Republic of Korea and Thailand has assumed added importance in view of the fact that reduction in poverty in developing world cannot wait for long.

Thailand

The case-study of Thailand presents an example of a country that succeeded in significant reduction in the incidence of poverty through sustained economic growth and through a policy orientation which generated employment opportunities for the poor. The rapid economic growth transformed the economy from agriculture based economy to manufacturing based and export oriented economy. The period between 1961 to 1996 witnessed a very high rate of economic growth. During this period Thailand registered improvements in almost all economic indicators such as Gross Domestic Product (GDP), per capita income, the level of exports and foreign investment. Between 1961 and 1996, Thailand implemented seven National Economy and Social Development Plans (NESDP). The average growth rate during this period was 7.8 per cent per year. It is a remarkable development-experience of Thailand that even though population increased from 33 million in 1966 to 60 million in 1996, per capita income increased from US$ 147 to US$ 3029. As a result of Thailand's spectacular economic growth and its progress in the reduction in poverty while growing at high rate, Thailand represented one of the East Asia's miracle economies.

Foreign trade played a major role in giving Thailand a sustained high rate of economic growth between 1961 to 1996.

During sixth and seventh plan, export grew @ 25.7 per cent and 44.2 per cent respectively.

The emergence of Thailand as an important player in the global trade can be assessed from the fact that the composition of exports registered major shift from primary products to manufacturing products such as computers, electrical applications, electronics etc. Export oriented growth resulted in economic prosperity during 1980s and 1990s. The expanding exports in manufacturing sector, especially exports of labour intensive products resulted in rapid expansion of employment opportunities. This had positive impact on the reduction in poverty because this increased income of people in the low income category. There were other important structural changes in the economy of Thailand between 1960 to 1996.

The share of agriculture sector was only 10.8 per cent in 1996 as compared to 38 per cent in 1960. It is also evident from Annexure—that the share of manufacturing sector in GDP rose from 13 per cent in 1960 to 31.4 per cent in 1996. In the export structure also, economic growth resulted in increasing share of manufacture. In 1985. Export of primary products accounted for 44.7 per cent of total exports. This share decreased to 16.5 per cent by 1995.

One of the important structural changes, which had a very significant impact on employment, was the shift of work-force from agriculture to manufacture sector. During 1960 to 1995, the share of agriculture in the total employment decreased from 84 per cent to 52 per cent. During the same period the share of manufactures in the employment increased from 3 per cent in 1960 to 13.4 per cent in 1995. The services sector also increased its share in employment from 13 per cent in 1960 to 34.5 per cent in 1995.

The high rate of economic growth in Thailand was accompanied by a notable reduction in poverty. According to the estimates by National Economic and Social Development Board, the incidence of poverty decreased from 32.6 per cent in 1988 to 11.4 per cent in 1996. In terms of number of poor people, there was a drastic reduction from 17.4 million poor persons in 1988 to 6.8 million persons in 1996.

Malaysia

Between 1970 and 1975, Malaysia succeeded in achieving

very fast reduction in the incidence of poverty. The incidence of poverty declined from 52.4 per cent in 1970 to 9.6 per cent in 1995. In Malaysia, among other factors, very significant factor contributing to the persistence of poverty was the lack of employment opportunity. The growing economy created jobs in many non-traditional sectors and that increased the income of the poor. With availability of more jobs, the share of household income from wages and salaries began to increase. The shift among rural household to salaried jobs was an important contributing factor in the reduction of poverty.

The reduction in poverty was also accompanied by improvements in social indicators. Malaysian economic development was marked by a high level of social development. In 1970, the combined primary and secondary enrollment was 62 per cent. In 1987, this increased to 78 per cent. By 1993, this ratio increased to 93 per cent for primary school.

Malaysia also achieved very high rate of success in providing health care to its population. In 1975, 62 per cent of the population had access to safe water. It rose to 78 per cent in 1990 and in 1994-95 it was about 90 per cent. Access to safe drinking water was nearly universal by 1994-95. In case of sanitation also, Malaysia achieved considerable improvement in expanding access of population to clean habitation. In 1980, 75 per cent of the population had adequate sanitation. In 1994-95, 94 per cent of the population had access to sanitation. Similarly by 1993, approximately 88 per cent of the population had access to health care services.

In health sector Malaysian achievement was remarkable. During sixth Malaysian development plan, almost 88 per cent of the urban poor and 77 per cent of the rural poor could access either a government or a private clinic within 9 kilometers. It was the policy initiatives in the New Economic Policy (NEP) since 1971, that contributed to achieving social development along with the process of economic growth. The New Economic Policy laid emphasis on rural development programmes, education and employment.

The development-strategy of Malaysia which was adopted in New Economic Policy (1970-90), played a major role in alleviating poverty. The rapid growth of export-oriented labour-intensive manufacturing sector provided employment for poor people. In the process of economic growth, the rapidly growing rural labour was absorbed in the urban industrial and service sector and that provided a major avenue for the reduction of rural poverty.

The tightening of the labour market in the late 1970s and early 1980s together with increased productivity of a more educated work-force led to increase in income of the poor people. Transfer of income to rural households by family members who migrated to urban areas played a significant role in mitigating poverty. In the 1990s, the rapid expansion of the economy led to the tightening of the labour market. The rate of unemployment fell from 5.1 per cent in 1990 to 2.8 per cent in 1995.

The success of Malaysia in promoting growth and alleviating poverty was the product of a very appropriate development strategy, which ensured growing income and social development. Malaysia has been regarded as a show-case of successful economic development. A notable feature of Malaysian development-experience in the context of poverty-alleviation is that while Malaysian economy is essentially market-economy, government involvement in poverty-alleviation has continued in providing basic needs and in the eradication of hard-core poverty. A Special Development Programme for Hard-Core Poor (DPHP) was designed to directly help the hard-core poor by the various development agencies.

The study of Malaysian development experience also shows that economic growth and poverty alleviation was closely related during growth process. The Malaysian economy has been growing at an average rate of 6.7 per cent since 1970s. During this period Malaysia also underwent remarkable transformation in the composition of Gross Domestic Product (GDP). In 1995 service sector accounted for 44.8 per cent of GDP and the share of agriculture was reduced from 29 per cent in 1970 to 13.9 per cent in 1995. A very high rate of economic growth which was sustained over several decades resulted in a very high rate of reduction in the incidence of poverty. Malaysia was able to reduce the incidence of poverty from 49.3 per cent in 1970 to 9.6 per cent in 1995. The accelerating economic growth was also accompanied by a choice of public policy that led to improvement in social indicators which have been analysed above.

Indonesia

Indonesia's economic growth has been spectacular and registered on average 7.6 per cent rate of economic growth per annum in 1990s. In 1995, its per capita income stood at US dollar 980. One of the salient features of Indonesian economic growth was that it was combined with rapid reduction in poverty.

In case of Indonesia, poverty declined mainly through increasing employment which resulted form rapid economic growth. Manufacturing employment grew annually at 5.6 per cent from 1971 to 1985 and then at 7.2 per cent from 1985 to 1990. Most of the jobs were created in labour-intensive export sector. Increasing employment along with increasing wages led to reduction in poverty.

In 1970, according to some estimates almost 60 per cent of the population, nearly 70 million people were living in absolute poverty in Indonesia. During two decades (1970 to 93), the proportion of the poor in Indonesia fell from 60 per cent to 14 per cent. The absolute number of poor fell from 67 million to 24 million. There were three major factors which contributed to reduction in poverty in Indonesia, viz., (i) improvement in agriculture; (ii) shift to labour intensive manufacturing; (iii) human development.

Between 1971-83, the average annual production of rice increased by 5.3 per cent per annum, nearly three times as fast as population growth. Average annual level of production increased from 8.3 million metric tons in 1955-60 to 23.5 million metric tons in 1980-84. With high labour intensities in agriculture sector, labour demand grew sharply and that further led to rising real wages in agriculture sector. This considerably increased income of the rural poor. The other important development in Indonesian economy in late 1980's was shift to labour intensive growth. Indonesia launched on several reforms in trade and investment sector and that resulted in growth in labour intensive export industries. Manufacturing output grew to about 12 per cent per annum in 1980's and this resulted in an increase in employment by 7 per cent per annum. This was one of the key factors in the decline in poverty.

The outward-oriented export-led industrialization resulted in dramatic increase in non-oil exports. After several years of stagnation in the early 1980's, private investment-both domestic and foreign, grew rapidly especially after 1988. Non-oil export grew from only dollar 5.9 Billion in 1985 to dollar 26.6 Billion in 1993. The share of non-oil exports in GDP grew three times during this period. Labour-intensive manufacturing grew fast which included garments, textiles, footwear, processed food, electrical products etc. These sectors absorbed labour at increasing rate and that raised the income of the people who were below poverty line. From the point of view of poverty-alleviation, the development-experience of Indonesia reflected a combination of factors which increased the absorption of labour in the lower income group. Along with growing employment, demand for workers rose faster than the growth in labour-supply. As labour-market tightened, this resulted in increasing real wages. This was probably the single most important factor in declining poverty in Indonesia. The growth in employment averaged between 4 per cent to 3 per cent in 1970s and 1980s which was higher than the rate of growth in labour-force. The employment scenario of Indonesia between 1970 to 1991 exhibited two important characteristics which contributed towards reduction in poverty. There was a shift in the distribution of employment from agriculture to service and to manufactures. In other words the proportion of formal sector employment increased. The other important change was that real wages increased both in agriculture and manufacturing sector. Between 1976 to 1988, real wages in agriculture improved by about 3.7 per cent per annum. Between 1970 to 1991, average manufacturing wages improved by about 5.5 per cent per annum. This trend in the real wages resulted in the movement of people from low income and under-employment situation to higher income and more productive jobs.

Indonesian experience of poverty-alleviation clearly shows that through public policy a country can achieve both economic growth and social development which is essential for removing income and human poverty. During the process of growth, Indonesia also achieved commendable improvement in social indicators. From 1960 to 1990, life-expectancy increased from 41 to 62 years. Infant mortality rate was reduced from 159 per thousand live births to 61 per thousand live births during this period. Adult illiteracy decreased from 61 per cent in 1960 to

23 per cent in 1990 and the percentage of primary enrollment during this period was raised from 71 to 118 per cent.

It is also a notable fact in Indonesian development-strategy that basic services was given priority in public policy. Indonesia allocated more than 80 per cent of total public expenditure to basic education. In the health sector also about 60 per cent of total public expenditure was allotted to rural health sector, family planning, and desease-control and child-health. It is worth mentioning that Indonesia attained near universal education by 1980s. Gross primary enrollment rate rose from 75 per cent to over 100 per cent between 1970–early 1980s. Indonesian experience also showed that if there is an appropriate policy-choice, economic growth can lead to minimizing human deprivations

The case-study of Indonesia very clearly underlines the contribution of human capital to growth and to reduction in poverty. Rapid rise in student enrolment reduced inequalities and that considerably contributed to major reduction in poverty. Wage differentials fell as rapid increases were made in all levels of education. The scarcity rent of education fell, and poor gained by moving from no or little education to increased earnings because of higher education. Then there were other spill-over effects of investment in human capital such as lower fertility rate, better health and better nutrition.

Republic of Korea

Republic of Korea achieved a very high rate of reduction in the incidence of poverty in a short span of time. In 1970, the incidence of poverty was at the level of 36.58 per cent. It was reduced to 7.17 per cent in 1990. A high degree of economic growth sustained through several decades generated conditions, which enabled Korea to significantly eliminate the scourge of poverty. Between 1972 to 1997 the Gross National Product grew at an average rate of 8.1 per cent. Per capita GNP increased from US dollar 253 in 1970 to US dollar ten thousand in 1996. There were three structural changes in Korean development-process which were closely related to poverty-alleviation. The changes include (i) the transformation of structure of production in the economy (ii) the transformation in the structure of employment (iii) the role of foreign trade.

These three structural changes were the outcome of labour-intensive and export-oriented industrial growth. The high rate of economic growth led to an increasing demand for labour. The rapid absorption of surplus labour raised the real wages. Wages in manufacturing sector grew at an average annual rate of 9.8 per cent between 1965 and 1973 and by 18 to 20 per cent between 1976 and 1979. By 1980, the unlimited supply of agricultural labour for manufacturing industry had come to an end. The economy also witnessed fundamental transformation in its composition. The share of agriculture in the Gross Domestic Product decreased from 27 per cent to less than 7.5 per cent during 1970 to 1997. There was spectacular increase in the trade sector. Industrial expansion increased labour demands that absorbed surplus labour or disguised unemployment in agriculture. This decreased the rate of absolute poverty. The rate of unemployment fell from 7.4 per cent in 1965 to less than 3 per cent in 1993.

A high degree of economic growth sustained through several years in continuation also contributed towards social development. Life expectancy at birth increased from 59.7 years in 1965 to 69.5 years in 1995. Infant mortality decreased from 61.8 deaths per one thousand life births in 1965 to 31.6 deaths in 1990. The population growth rate per annum also declined from 2.3 per cent in 1965 to 1 per cent per annum in 1990.

Apart from the expanding employment opportunities generated by rapid economic growth and industrialization, human resource development played a very important role in the success of poverty-reduction in Korea. Formal education and skill-training are the most effective means of preventing the transmission of poverty from generation to generation. In a developing economy, to reduce poverty it is necessary that opportunities should be generated for all individuals so that they can participate in the growth-process. Human resource development has played a critical role in Korea's rapid economic growth and poverty-alleviation. Korea accorded priority to education in its public expenditure policy. Through the expanding education, the demand for skilled workers was met and economic growth did not suffer because of lack of skilled labour. The other important policy which helped in poverty alleviation was successful implementation of land reforms. The land reform carried out by government abolished tenancy and the distribution of land holdings was equalized on the basis of "land to the tiller principle". The implementation of the Land Reforms Act of 1949 resulted in significant decline in the proportion of tenant farms, which decreased, from 42 per cent of farm population in 1947 to 5.2 per cent in 1964. Since the majority of the population was in agriculture, it resulted in substantial improvement in living standards. Land reforms in Korea was vital to poverty alleviation because it led to the distribution of assets which is a necessary condition for removing mass poverty. The decline in inequality which resulted from land reform stimulated Korean economic growth. This also supported the hypothesis that greater equality in the distribution of assets which leads to higher income for the poor will increase the rate of economic growth. The government also paid attention to improving agricultural terms of trade and that raised the income of the farmers. Another major policy shift was the launching of New Community Movement (NCM). This policy helped in carrying out integrated rural development projects. Through these projects the income of the poor was raised and the degree of deprivations was reduced.

In addition to lifting the poor above poverty line, Korea also ensured fulfillment of basic needs of the poor. In some of the areas such as the access to safe drinking water, the coverage increased from 33 per cent in 1970 to 83 per cent in 1995. Similarly by 1995, medical insurance covered almost 98 per cent of population. In education the coverage was almost 100 per cent by 1995.

The success of Korea in achieving high rate of poverty alleviation was closely related to the pattern of economic growth which was followed. When Korea embarked on economic development, the development-targets included light industry such as textile, footwear, plywood, fertilizers and other labour intensive consumer goods. Even for the development of infrastructure, Korea applied labour intensive strategy in the initial stage of development. With the result, labour absorption was rapid enough to reduce unemployment from 7.3 per cent in 1965 to 4.1 per cent in 1975. This strategy also helped Korea in providing jobs to unskilled workers and that directly reduced the number of poor. By 1995 the rate of unemployment in Korea was not more than 2 per cent.

Important lessons emerge from the case-studies of Malaysia, Indonesia and Republic of Korea who achieved spectacular success in reducing poverty. The aspect of East Asian policy that most contributed to equitable growth was government financing and provisioning of basic social services. In the Republic of Korea for example, government finance accounted for almost 100 per cent of the direct cost of primary education. Even in case of tertiary education, the government spent approximately 50 per cent of the total expenditure. The importance of public policy in the eradication of poverty is very much underlined in the development-experience of East Asian countries.

A very important lesson from the experience of those countries who were successful in the elimination of poverty is that to meet the objective of reducing both income and human poverty it is essential that the pattern of growth should the such that increases the capabilities of the poor and meets the basic needs.

It may be pointed out that poverty eradication through "trickle-down" is a very slow and uncertain process. The rate of economic growth by itself may not influence poverty reduction. It is therefore necessary that the policies relevant for poverty-reduction should be so oriented that it attacks the poverty directly by meeting the basic needs of the population. The two important aspects of human deprivation in a poor country which are instrumental in perpetuating poverty include lack of education and lack of health care.

Education directly influences the process of poverty-reduction. Education is important because it enables poor to participate in non-agricultural sector where skilled labour is required. Education of poor facilitates movement into non-farm rural work and migration to towns and also to service sector. In Korea for example, education was very important source of reduction in earning-differential among workers between 1970 and 1990.

The provisioning of health services to the poor is equally important for raising the capabilities of the poor. State can provide affordable health services to the poor. It has been amply demonstrated in the case of East Asian countries such as Indonesia, Korea, Malaysia, Thailand that increasing expenditure on health by the government improved the welfare of the people and hence helped in reducing poverty. It is also important to note that the pattern of economic growth that was accompanied by wide coverage of education and health services enables the poor to avail the opportunities that are created in the process of economic growth.

The East Asian countries in their fight against poverty have also shown that employment was central to reducing poverty in East Asia. The economic growth in these countries created employment opportunities in the non-farm sector and that absorbed low income poor people. It may be pointed out that in the late 1950s, less than 30 per cent, Malaysian work-force was in wage-paying industrial and service jobs. By the end of 1980s, the share of the work-force in industries and services rose to approximately 60 per cent. Similarly in Korea, agricultural employment fell from 50 per cent of the work-force in 1970 to 20 per cent in 1980. In East Asia, growth in rural non-farm employment-opportunities has been a major feature of rural income growth. This had cumulative effect on other variables of economic growth. Higher agricultural income increased the demand for goods and services and that helped in financing investment in off-farm industries. In case of China also rural non-farm employment grew by 130 million jobs between 1980 and 1999.

Chile

In the study of relationship between economic growth and reduction in poverty, the experience of some developing countries in other regions such as Latin America and Africa is also of crucial importance. In Latin America, Chile achieved considerable reduction in poverty in a relatively short span of time. Between 1985 and 1997, Chile's Gross Domestic Product (GDP) grew at an annual average of 7 per cent, more than double the average rate of economic growth of 3.3 per cent in the region. Along with the accelerating economic growth, Chile achieved substantial reduction in the proportion of people below the line of poverty. In past ten years or so poverty fell drastically in Chile. The percentage of the population living with per capita income below the poverty line fell from 45 per cent in 1987 to less than 25 per cent in 1996. Chile's success in reducing poverty is comparable to the performance of East Asian countries viz., Korea, Indonesia, Malaysia, China etc. Chile's policies reflected a combination of priority on economic growth and social development. In case of Chile, public expenditure policy played a very important role in improving the quality of life through meeting basic needs of the population. In 1990s, Chile's social spending grew and was well targeted towards the poorest 40 per cent of the population. Social expenditure was concentrated on providing public goods and services such as health care and education. In providing the basic needs of the population, Chile ranked third among developing countries in human poverty index of the UNDP 1997. The Human Poverty Index of the UNDP measures longevity, access to basic knowledge and minimum level of consumption. The ranking of Chile in the UNDP HPI index reflected its success in the fulfillment of basic needs of the population along with achieving very high rate of economic growth which could be compared to the rapid growth in the East Asian countries.

The study of diverse development experience of developing countries brings to focus important aspects of policy-choice to eliminate poverty in the developing world. The success of poverty-alleviation in East Asian countries and Chile has established close link between the rate of economic growth and rate of reduction in poverty. It has also shown that a meaningful dent in poverty which can be effective in minimizing the deprivations suffered by poor people, can be made only when economic growth is accompanied by the social development. In all the cases studied so far. It has been evident that a country that follows public policy to meet basic needs of society, succeeds in eliminating both income poverty and human poverty. The experience of some developing countries however also shows that the country can achieve success in minimizing human deprivation even in a situation when it goes through the process of low rate of economic growth. In other words a country may not give its people very high rate of economic growth but can fulfill their basic needs depending on the public policy that the country adopts. The case of Sri Lanka stands out as an illustration of a country which has succeeded in attacking poverty primarily through the channel of meeting basic needs.

Sri Lanka

The social indicators of Sri Lanka underline the fact that a country can achieve social and human development at any level of economic growth. In 1991, Sri Lanka's crude death rate was 6 per one thousand. It had achieved life-expectancy rate of 72.5 years. Its infant mortality rate stood at 17.5 and maternal mortality rate stood at 4 per thousand births respectively. It had also achieved very high rate of literacy and that was 87 per cent. The social indicators of Sri Lanka which reflect of degree of fulfillment of basic needs stood much higher than the average rate achieved by developing countries in Asia, Africa and Latin America.

The improvement in the social indicators, which has been analysed above, is the outcome of the policies followed by Sri Lanka right from 1950s in the sectors, which included health and education. There were three important areas viz., education, health and nutrition to which Sri Lanka gave priority and made the access affordable both in physical and financial terms to its people. In health sector, food subsidies played very vital role. The provision of free education and health services also led to declining rate of population-growth and that was positive factor for economic development.

In fight against poverty, the experience of Botswana in Africa shows that social and human development is of paramount importance. Botswana was able to improve its social indicators at much higher rate then other developing countries in Africa region and also in other regions. The improvement in social indicators included (i) significant reduction in less than five mortality rate and infant mortality rate. Between 1970 – 1990, Life-expectancy rose from 46 to 63 years during 1970-90, Adult literacy rate and primary schools enrollment doubled during this period.

Botswana

Botswana achieved almost universal primary education and improvement in health-indicators. Botswana's poverty-profile in 1990s also demonstrated that even though a country may not succeed in alleviating income-poverty, it can achieve a very high level of social development and can succeed in expanding the capabilities of poor people. The case-study of

Botswana leads to the conclusion that it is the choice of development strategy on which depends the effectiveness of economic growth in reducing poverty. The poor in Botswana enjoyed very high-level social provision, which included education, clean water and health care. Social expenditure in Botswana accounted for 35 per cent of public expenditure between 1976 and 1995. From 1972 onwards expenditure on health and education continued to rise. Their combined share of total public spending rose from 10 per cent in 1972 to 22 per cent in 1976. Health alone accounted for 4 to 5 per cent of total public expenditure. Botswana's social development experience stands out as one of the most successful policy framework leading to minimizing human deprivation among the people in the developing world.

Costa Rica

Costa Rica achieved radical improvements in social indicators which compared with the attainment in social development by industrialised countries. There were remarkable improvement in social indicators such as life expectancy, education, infant mortality rate etc. Between 1995 and 1990, the infant mortality rate was reduced by 84 per cent and illiteracy was reduced by 67 per cent. Malnutrition declined by 71 per cent. The incidence of poverty also declined drastically. According to human development indicators developed by UNDP, Costa Rica's level of human development rose from medium to high during 1980.

The high level of human and social development achieved by Costa Rica is clearly demonstrated when we compare its social indicators with developed countries and some other developing countries. For example, in 1992, Costa Rica's infant mortality rate was 14 per one thousand compared to 13 per one thousand in the industrialized countries. In case of other important indicators of human and social development, i.e., life expentancy, the achievement of Costa Rica was comparable to that of developed countries. In 1992 life expectancy at birth in Costa Rica was 76 years, which was equal to the rate of life expectancy in many industrialised countries. In the field of human development also, the achievement of Costa Rica was remarkable. Adult literacy in Costa Rica was 93 per cent which compares very closely with the level of adult literacy achieved by industrialized countries.

In the two sectors, which constitute the foundations for human and social development, viz., education and health, Costa Rica made tremendous progress by following appropriate social policies. In the health sector, universal health care coverage was included in the nation's constitution. Wage-earners with medium to high incomes were included in the obligatory social security system which included health insurance. Per capita expenditure on health annually increased @ 8 per cent. Almost 84 per cent of the population was covered by the health insurance schemes. By 1990, 93 per cent of the population received piped water. In the public financing, health care was given priority and by 1990 approximately, Costa rica spent 56 dollars per person on health. A remarkable feature of Costa Rica's social policy was the universalization of health care. This was made possible by widening health insurance coverage to cover non-wage earning workers who wished to join programme on their own account. Primary health care was the corner stone of Costa Rica's health policy. The government-established rural health programme in 1973 and in 1976 community health programme was established. By the end of 1970s, the rural health programme covered 60 per cent of the rural population. The community health programme covered 60 per cent of the urban population and reduced the gap between the poor and the rich in access to health care. During 1970s as a result of widening coverage of health care, life expectancy rose by 8 years. The other positive impact of the universalization of health care was that the infant mortality rate dropped by 70 per cent during a single decade. In 1980 this reached 20 per one thousand.

In education sector as well, Costa Rica made tremendous progress by increasing the coverage of access to education by the population. By 1990 in primary education the enrollment was more than 100 per cent and in the secondary education it averaged at 60 per cent. Per capita expenditure on education was at the level of 57 dollars per person by 1990.

Costa Rica also launched on several institutional innovations, which ensured a very high level of social development for the population. A number of institutions were created by the government to assist poor. The government created specialised institutions to handle the country's potable water supply. Access to basic services such as water and electricity was expanded. Between 1950 and 1970 the percentage of population that had running water rose from 53 per cent to 75 per cent and the percentage of homes with electricity increased from 40 per cent to 65 per cent.

One of the ongoing debates among economists and policy-makers in deciding policy-package for reduction of poverty has centered around the issue whether a developing country can wait for "trickle – down" effect of economic growth to ensure fulfillment of basic needs of education, health, literacy, sanitation, drinking water etc. or this should be provided by government through public policy. The experience of the East Asian and of some other developing countries such as Botswana, Sri Lanka has clearly demonstrated that human and social development is a necessary factor in reduction in poverty and also it impacts positively the process of economic growth. The very important lesson of East Asian model of the development is that human resource development results in equity and also enhances economic growth in the developing countries. It is through education that poor acquires earning capacity and it is through the fulfillment of their basic needs such as health, sanitation etc., their capabilities increase. The case-study also demonstrates that a developing country can raise the level of social and human development even though the country has not achieved a very high level of growth in per capita income. It is important to note from the case studies that the choice of policy is of crucial importance for reduction in human poverty in the developing countries.

CHAPTER III

Breaking Vicious Circle of Poverty in Economies Trapped in the Low Level-Income-Equilibrium

The case-study of selected developing countries in East Asia, Latin America and in Africa brought to focus the interaction between Economic growth and poverty. The success of the developing countries who achieved reduction in poverty, underlined the strong link between the rate and pattern of economic growth and the elimination of poverty. There are a number of countries spread over in Africa and Asia where because of very weak economic growth, poverty has persisted during last five decades of development. These countries are grouped under Least Developed Countries (LDCs) and comprise of 49 countries. Most of the countries numbering 33 in this group belong to Sub-Saharan Africa. Please see Annexure III-1. The poverty-profile of these countries has assumed important dimensions for international economic co-operation. A survey of poverty-profile of the Least Developed Countries (LDCs) shows high degree of intensity of poverty in terms of income and also it shows a very high level of sufferings in terms of human deprivations.

According to the UNCTAD report entitled "The Least Developed Countries 2000 Report", on an average, 44 per cent of the population have a per capita income of under one US dollar a day and about 75 per cent have a per capita income of less than two dollars a day. The percentage of people who have to survive at less than a dollar per day is very high in some countries which are listed at Annexure III-2. Some of the countries such as Burkina Faso, Central African Republic, Madagascar, Zambia have more than 60 per cent of the population surviving on less than a dollar per day.

The persistence of low income for last several years has been the key factor responsible for considerably high degree of poverty in the Least Developed Countries (LDCs) especially in Sub-Saharan Africa. The UNCTAD Secretariat calculations at Annexure-III.3 reveals the widening gap in GDP per capita between other developing countries and the Least Developed Countries. In 1997, for LDCs, the GNP per capita (PPP) was at the level of 1343$ as against 4.598$ for Developing Countries.

Since 1980s, most of the LDCs especially the countries belonging to Sub-Saharan Africa suffered from faltering economic growth which led to declining income. The LDCs registered on an average 2.2 per cent annual rate of growth between 1982-1990. Between 1990-1994, these countries grew at the rate of 2 per cent per annum. Since 1995, the LDCs picked-up higher rate of economic growth which has been on average 3.2 per cent. It is worth pointing out that higher aggregate rate of economic growth after 1995 was mainly the result of better economic performance of Bangladesh. Excluding Bangladesh there was not much improvement in the performance of LDCs during 1995-1998. The other point which needs to be explained is that even though LDCs attained on an average higher rate of economic growth in 1990s, it could not make dent in poverty because of high rate of population growth. When we take into account the high rate of population growth, GDP per capita could grow only at 0.9 per cent per annum during 1990-1998.

The growth-performance of the Least Developed Countries (LDCs) clearly shows that high intensity of poverty among the LDCs as compared to other developing countries is closely related with the rate of economic growth. As will be observed from Annexure III-4, very low per capita GDP since 1980s resulted in a situation in which poor people could not cross international poverty line of US$ one per day. The poverty situation was further aggravated for Sub-Saharan African Countries who registered negative per capita GDP at – 0.9 per cent during 1980-1990 and at – 0.4 per cent during 1992-1998.

The continued low rate of GDP growth and negative growth in per capita GDP for most of the African LDCs resulted in the lack of resources for social and human development in these countries. The people not only suffered from income poverty but also suffered from the lack of the fulfillment of basic needs. The high degree of human deprivations suffered by poor people in these countries is reflected from the following social indicators.

Social Indicators for the LDCs and other DCs

	Year	*LDCs*	*DCs*
Mortality rate, under-five (per 1,000 live births	1997	108	65
Life expectancy at birth (Years)	1990-1995	49	62
Hospital bed (per 1,000 population)	1990	1.1	4.8
Physicians (Per 1,000 population)	1990	0.1	1.6
Adult literacy rate (age 15 and above)	1995	48.9	81.4
Gross school enrolment (per cent)			
Primary	1995	72.0	100.0
Secondary	1995	16.0	65.0
Tertiary	1995	1.6	17.7
Telephone mainlines (per 1,000 population)	1998	4.0	58.0a
Telephone Average cost of local call ($ per three minutes)	1997	0.1	0.05

Source : LDCs Report—2000.

The Table above shows that the LDCs have not been able to meet the basic needs of their people in health and education which are the two important determinants of standard of living. The life- expectancy at 49 years as compared with 62 years for the developing countries reflects lack of health care. Similarly very high rate of child-mortality indicates the lack of access to adequate medical facilities. In the field of education also the LDCs have failed in attaining comparable level of literacy. For LDCs the adult literacy rate at the rate of only 48.9 per cent very poorly compares with 81.4 per cent for the developing countries.

A brief survey of social indicators in respect of African LDCs who form the largest group among LDCs, points out to widening gap between the fulfillment of basic needs for the people living in these countries and the level of human and social development attended by the developing countries.

It has been estimated that out of approximately 580 million people living in Sub-Saharan Africa (33 out of 49 LDCs), 124 million die before attaining the age of forty years. It has also been estimated that during the period 1992 to 1995, approximately 205 million people out of 500 million had no access to health-services. It is alarming to note that during 1990-1995, almost half of the population in the region had no access to safe drinking water. During this period, Sub-Saharan region also suffered from very high degree of illiteracy as approximately 139 million youth were illiterate.

The poverty-profile of Sub-Saharan African Countries which accounts for 33 out of 49 LDCs, shows that between 1987-1998, the number of absolute poor increased from 217 million to 219 million. This trend is in sharp contrast to the changing face of poverty in other developing countries. During the same period in East Asia and pacific, the number of absolute poor decreased from 251 million in 1987 to 278 million in 1998. The table at Annexure-III.5 shows the changing face of poverty in the developing world. The Poverty-profile of Sub-Saharan Africa indicates that both in terms of income poverty and in terms of human poverty there was no progress in 1980s and 1990s. In 21st century therefore the eradication of poverty in Sub-Saharan Africa throws up major challenge for the international community. The challenges are basically two fold : first to increase the rate of economic growth by narrowing the resource-gap and second, new policy initiatives to ensure that rising income is translated into improved welfare. The Development – experience in some countries shows that in spite of higher income per capita, some countries have not been able to increase rate of life - expectancy. It has also been seen in past that there is a strong relation between life - expectancy and per capita income . The empirical evidence shows that with same per capita income some countries in Sub-Saharan Africa when compared with other developing countries have attained different levels of life – expectancy. For example : Nigeria and Vietnam have same per capita income but Nigeria has attained 54 years of life expectancy whereas Vietnam has attained 68 years of the life expectancy. Similarly Zambia and Nicargua have same per capita income but Zambia has attained only 43 years of life expectancy while Nicargua has attained 68 years of life expectancy. The International comparisons in almost all social indicators such as life expectancy at birth, infant-mortality, under nourishment, illiteracy shows that Sub-Saharan Africa has lagged behind in human and social development. This gap has been widening during last four decades.

The study of the economies of LDCs reflects very weak influence that economic growth has on the eradication of poverty of these countries. Since LDC 1980s, and continuing through 1990s, there has emerged a gap between per capita income of growth of other developing countries and that of LDCs. During 1990-1998, other developing countries have registered 3.6 per cent per capita income growth while LDCs have registered only 0.5 per cent per capita income growth during this period. In case of 33 countries in Sub-Saharan Africa, per capita income has been continuously falling and they have experienced an absolute reduction in their standard of living.

For a comprehensive analysis of poverty in the LDCs, it is important to identify the factors which contribute to stagnation in the economies of the LDCs. The UNCTAD, through its various reports such as Annual Trade and Development Reports, and Least Developed Countries (LDCs). Reports has brought to focus structural imbalances which inhibit process of economic development in these countries. The factors which have been identified in these reports include the lack of domestic resources for investment, the high degree of dependence of LDCs economies on the export earnings from primary commodities, falling terms of trade of primary commodities, huge external resource gap and increasing external indebtedness etc.

For most of the LDCs, the main source of revenue is from export of primary goods. Economic growth in Sub-Saharan African Countries has been subject to movements in terms of trade. After a phase of declining terms of trade between 1988 and 1993, there was a slight upturn in 1994-1995 and after 1998 again commodity prices registered falling trend. The table showing changes in the terms of the trade for the export of primary goods is at Annexure-III.6. During 1998-99, the index of commodity price fell by 30 per cent and this led to a significant decline in the GDP of LDCs, especially of the countries in the Sub-Saharan region.

While poor economic growth continues to remain the primary factor in reducing poverty, there are also other structural bottlenecks such as high rate of population growth, large share of agriculture in the GDP, low level of industrialization, low level of human development and of socio-economic infrastructure; that limit the prospect of poverty reduction in the LDCs. The development-effort of LDCs is often disrupted by their vulnerability to natural disasters and external shocks. It has been estimated that during 1975-99, there were 1138 instances of natural disasters which affected 6 hundred million people. The study of the development-experience of the LDCs clearly shows that for economic development, access to external resources is but indispensable. The domestic resources for the development are not sufficient even to meet critically minimum requirements of investment for economic growth. In these economies where a large part of population survives at near subsistence level of consumption, private consumption takes a major share of GNP and leaves small amount of resources to finance development. All these factors have resulted in a very high degree of external resources dependence for the LDCs. The intensity of their dependence on external resources is explained in the table at Annexure III-7. It has been recognized that if LDCs have to escape from the low level equilibrium trap, they need much higher inflow of external resources. The present rate of economic growth is not a viable proposition for reduction of poverty among the LDCs.

It is important to note that the external resource-gap for investment in case of Sub-Saharan African LDCs has been almost 100 per cent between 1980-1998. To achieve international development goal of reducing poverty by half by the year 2015, massive investment will be required according to the estimate of the Economic Commission For Africa. The ECA also estimated that at least 7 per cent annual rate of economic growth must be attained by the 32 African LDCs, if they have to meet the target of reducing poverty by the year 2015. Higher rate of economic growth as advised by ECA will require doubling of the rate of the investment and also doubling of the inflow of external resources.

The above analysis points out to the need for increase in external resources for the LDCs. As explained in Annexure III-8. The 1990s have however witnessed a disturbing trend of declining capital inflows for the LDCs. Long term net capital inflows into LDCs have declined by above 25 per cent since 1990.

In 1991, the level of such inflows was dollar 14.2 billion which came down to dollar 10.4 billion in 1998. The declining trend in the capital inflow in the LDCs is in contrast with the trend of increasing capital inflows in other developing countries in 1990s. As compared with other developing countries, official financing is of much greater importance for the LDCs. During 1983-1989, the share of official finance in total capital inflow was about 89 per cent for LDCs. On the other hand for other developing countries, private capital inflows accounted for more than 80 per cent of the total capital inflow in 1990s. The share of Foreign Direct Investment (FDI) has been also falling for the LDCs. In 1990s FDI accounted for only 1.4 per cent of the capital inflows for the LDCs.

To fight poverty in the LDCs, external resources need to be augmented on priority basis. As we have seen above private capital inflow has been very sluggish for the LDCs and for their external resources, official aid assumes relatively much more importance than private capital. However, recently it has been seen that DAC countries have failed in meeting their commitments of ODA to the LDCs. UNCTAD report entitled "Least Developed Countries Report 2000" has pointed out that aid flows to LDCs as measured by the share of net ODA disbursement in donor's GNP, have almost halved in the 1990s. At the start of decade, the total ODA of DAC countries to LDCs stood at 0.09 per cent of their combined GNP, whilst in 1998 it was down to 0.05 per cent. In many cases, special targets for ODA to LDCs were not fulfilled. These targets were set in the Programme of Action For the LDCs for 1990s. This has been a major concern for the international community and the attention of the donor countries has been drawn towards this problem in the United Nations Conference on the LDCs.

Apart from insufficient inflows of capital, especially in the form of long-term credit and grants, the majority of LDCs continue to be burdened with a serious debt overhang. In 1999, outstanding external debt of the LDCs as a share of their aggregate GDP amounted to 89 per cent, and the average ratio of debt service paid (as opposed to scheduled payments) to exports was 15 per cent. A number of countries continued to be unable to meet their obligations in full, accumulating further arrears on scheduled payments.

Rising level of external debt puts further constraints on the growth-prospects of the LDCs. In 1976, only 2 out of 28 LDCs had external debt to GDP ratios of over 50 per cent and external debt to export ratios higher than 200 per cent. By 1982 over half of the LDCs had reached external indebtedness of the level. The nineties also witnessed trend towards increasing the stock of external debt. The nominal value of total external debt increased from dollar 121.2 billion in 1990 to dollar 150.4 billion in 1998. This corresponded to an estimated 101 per cent of their combined GNP. Half of the debt was concentrated in six countries—Angola, Bangladesh, the Democratic Rep. Of the Congo, Ethiopia, Sudan. While the stock of external debt kept on rising for LDCs, the debt servicing capacity of the LDCs deteriorated in 1990s. In 1998, the earnings from export-earnings declined and that led to the worserning of debt-servicing capacity of the LDCs. Total debt-service paid by LDCs as a whole amounted to dollar 4.4 billion in 1998.

The debt-burden siphoned off most of resources for economic growth and that further contributed towards perpetuation of poverty among the LDCs. Increasing burden of debt and of debt-service payments called for new and innovative mechanisms for debt-relief to the LDCs. The traditional mechanisms for debt-relief for LDCs included the re-scheduling of principal and interest-payments with paris club creditors on either concessional or non-concessional terms, forgiveness of bilateral ODA debt by converting concessional loans into grants, reduction of commercial debt through IDA debt-reduction facility etc. In addition IMF also provided concessional financing to reduce debt-burden. Although these traditional debt-relief mechanisms alleviated the debt-burden of many LDCs, the overhang of debt problems continued in 1990s.

The new policy initiative to provide debt relief was taken by the international community. Under new framework of policies, additional measures of debt relief were designed for countries which were assessed by the donors to fall under the category of Heavily Indebted Poor Countries (HIPC). The HIPC initiative which was introduced in 1996, widened the coverage of the types of debts which are eligible for relief to include multi-lateral debt. The initiative also set an explicit target for debt-sustainability. A country is considered to have achieved external debt-sustainability if it can meet current and future external debt-service obligations in full without recourse to debt relief, debt-re-scheduling or accumulation of arrears . Under HPIC-I, the target for debt sustainability was set as a threshold ratio of the present value of debt to exports or to government revenue. Under HPIC-I, the maximum ratio of present value of debt to export considered sustainable was initially set at 200-250 per cent. In G-8 Cologne summit in June 1999. these limits were lowered to fixed level of 150 per cent. The maximum sustainable level for the ratio of present value of debt to fiscal revenue was also lowered from 280 per cent to 250 per cent. The threshold required to qualify for HIPC assistance under the new criterion were also lowered from 40 to 30 per cent in the export to GDP ratio and 20 to 15 per cent in the case of revenue to GDP ratio. The new initiative is known as the Enhanced HIPC.

Under HIPC–II, creditors are expected to share the reduction in the future debt-service obligations required to bring the present value of debt to exports and of debt to revenue ratio down to sustainable levels according to their share of the present value of the debt at decision point. Under HIPC–II, new sources and mechanism for financing debt relief were also introduced. These include IMF gold sales, setting of the HIPC. Trust Fund to which bilateral donors may contribute to help the multilateral institution.

With the enhancement of the HIPC initiative, there has been a significant change in the nature and extent of conditionality attached to debt relief. These changes are very significant for the reduction of poverty in the LDCs.

Under HIPC–II a country has to fulfill following conditions to get debt relief :

(a) It has to establish a three year record of good performance under IMF and World Bank adjustment programmes before the decision point.

(b) The completion-point in HIPC–II, is floating. It can be reached in less than three years if a country can implement reforms. Or it can take longer.

(c) The achievement of the completion-point is conditional on achieving a macro-economic position conducive to sustainable growth and poverty-reduction.

The key change in the content of policy conditionality is that goal of poverty reduction has been added to existing policy-conditionality . Policy reforms under HIPC–II have to be geared towards the achievement of poverty-reduction objectives and also towards the implementation of social development policies. In the new orientation towards poverty-reduction, the ESAF has been replaced by Poverty Reduction and Growth Facility (PRGF), which became effective since November 1999. The purpose of new facility is to support those programmes which foster durable growth and lead to higher living standard and poverty reduction.

The central goal of the enhanced HIPC initiative is to strengthen the link between debt relief and poverty reduction. This also provides incentives for governments to adopt pro-poor economic reforms through the new policy conditionalties. It also seeks to ensure that there sources released from debt-relief will be channeled into increased social expenditure on health and education. In meeting basic needs of people, the LDCs are seriously constrained by increasing debt-service payments. The burden of debt-service payments on the resource-availability for social development is explained in the table at Annexure III-9. This shows that for Tanzania, Mali and for some other countries listed in the table, the payment of debt-service far exceeds the expenditure on social services. It is therefore evident that unless the burden of debt is alleviated, LDCs will not be able to attain reduction in human poverty. Their performance in terms of attaining some of the international development goals is shown in Annexure III-10. It is evident from the performance in respect of infant mortality and primary school enrollment that there has emerged a wide gap between the International Development goals and present level of attaining these goals by the LDCs.

The persistence of poverty in the LDCs which include 33 Sub-Saharan African Countries present serious challenge for the international community in achieving the international development goal of halving poverty by 2015. In its review of progress in the eradication of poverty during the decade (1997-2006) the United Nations have observed that region-wise, the profile of poverty has worsened in Sub-Saharan Africa in 1990s. The review of the progress in the implementation of the first

United Nations Decade For the Eradication of poverty was documented in the report of the Secretary-General of the United Nations. The report "inter-allia" points out to the increasing number of population living on less than dollar one per day, has increased in Sub-Saharan Africa from 217.2 million in 1987 to 219.9 million in 1998. In terms of human sufferings and deprivations the prevalence of poverty at this level has led to the building-up of a global consensus to create conditions which can enable these countries to escape from poverty.

It has been recognized by the international community that without accelerating the rate of economic growth in LDCs, it may not be possible to reduce the number of poor people and to enable them to achieve minimum level of social development. This recognition of the need to ensure higher rate of the economic growth has been manifested in the deliberation of the United Nations Conferences on LDCs since 1981. In the first United Nations Conference on LDCs in Paris in 1981, the international community adopted "New Programme of Action" for the 1980s. The Second Conference was held in Paris in September 1990 to review the progress in the implementation of Programme Of Action. The conference issued a Declaration called "Paris Declaration and Programme of Action" for the L.D.Cs in 1990s. International community thereby committed to arrest the deterioration in the development of LDCs. In a mid-term review of implementation of Action Programme in 1995, it was concluded that the LDCs· continued to be marginalized in global economy. In 1997 the United Nations General Assembly decided to convene the Third United Nations Conference on LDCs to assess the result of the Programme of Action during the 1990s and to review the implementation of international support measures, particularly in the areas of Official Development Assistance, investments, debt, trade and also to consider the adoption of policies for sustainable development of LDCs and their progressive integration into the world economy.

The Third United Nations Conference on the LDCs was held in Brussels from 14th to 20th may 2001. In a message issued for the conference Secretary General Kofi Annan called for a "Global New Deal" to help the dis-advantaged regions to catch up with the developed world. In his message he also said "at stake, quite simply; in the future of these poorest of the poor, is the well-being of the entire community".

The conference adopted a political declaration in which 193 participating countries committed themselves to the eradication of poverty in the world's poorest countries and to the improvement of the quality of lives of more than 600 million people living in these countries. The conference adopted an Action Programme for the next decade which addresses development assistance, debt cancellation, investment etc. The Programme of Action for the decade 2001-2010 calls for initiative to arrest marginalisation of LDCs. The participating governments committed to reverse the declining trends of ODA and also commited to the speedy implementation of the Enhanced Heavily Indebted Poor Countries (HIPC-II) initiative of the World Bank and IMF. The relevant details of Action programmes are summarised at Annexure III-13.

The development partners agreed to, implement the OECD recommendations to "untie" aid to LDCs and to provide aid without conditions. They also agreed to implement a number of commitments previously made in Paris : those providing more than 0.2 per cent of their gross national product as ODA to LDCs agreed to continue; others, providing 0.15 per cent of gross national product, agreed to reach 0.2 per cent expeditiously. Those donors who had committed themselves to the 0.15 per cent target reaffirmed their commitment and undertook to achieve the target within the next five years.

The participants recognized that LDC's "integration into the World economy is a necessary precondition for long-term sustainability of poverty reduction". Development partners also agreed to improve preferential market access for LDCs by working towards the objective of duty-free and quota-free market acess for all LDC products in the markets of developed countries. They also agreed to implement in full the special and differential measures for LDCs, as contained in the Final Act of the Uruguay Round, while considering new measures for LDCs as part of future multilateral trade negotiations. The participants also agreed to support the diversion programme of LDC's exports.

Trade expansion is crucial for augmenting rate of economic growth and for the eradication of poverty in most of the countries in Africa who are trapped in low income equilibrium. Most of these countries depend on foreign trade as the main source of the revenue. The diminishing share of The Least Development Countries (LDCs) in International Trade has been a major factor in the stagnation suffered by these countries. The third UN conference on LDCs which devoted attention to the eradication of poverty, laid down special emphasis on the promotion of trade and prescribed policy-measures to increase export of these countries. Relevant extracts from the Actions Programme adopted by the Third UN conference on LDCs outlining the policy-initiatives for increasing trade are Annexed at Annexure III-14.

On the basis of its estimates of growth elasticity of poverty in Africa, the Economic Commission of Africa (ECA) (1999) has provided estimates of necessary growth and hence investment requirements in various part of Africa for achieving the poverty reduction targets. According to those estimates, to achieve the poverty reduction target the Sub-Saharan African countries (which comprise 32 LDCs) should be able to sustain on average of GDP growth rate of over 7 per cent per annum. With the prevailing savings propensities and investment efficiency, ECA estimates that at least a doubling of investment rates, and hence a more than doubling of the inflow of external resources, are necessary for Sub-Saharan Africa on average to achieve the OECD poverty reduction targets.

Such projections are, of course, highly sensitive to the assumptions made about investment efficiency and savings rates. However, on the basis of different assumptions regarding the marginal savings rates and investment efficiency, UNCTAD estimates external resource requirements of between 50 and 150 per cent higher than the existing flows in the short run in Sub-Saharan Africa, for escaping the low-level equilibrium trap and achieving self-sustained growth rates of 6 per cent a year. Such average projections for Sub-Saharan Africa are likely to be relevant to most African and Asian LDCs that have low savings rates and are caught in the low-level equilibrium trap.

The Poverty-Profile of the LDCs as analysed above points out to the policy challenges in meeting the International Development goals which have been identified by the international community. These goals have been tabulated at Annexure III-12. The present level of per capita income of the LDCs and the trend in their per capita income growth may not enable these economies who are trapped in the low income equilibrium, to attend the goals and targets related to the reduction of income and human poverty within the time-bound frame work.

According to the UNCTAD calculations, at Annexure III-11 the level of dollar 900 per capita income per annum is required to graduate these countries from the category of LDCs to the developing countries. The empirical evidence shows that only at a relatively higher level of per capita income, a country is able to reduce the degree of intensity of poverty. It has been projected that on the basis of current trends in economic growth, only one of the LDCs, i.e., LESOTHO will be able to cross this limit of dollar 900 per capita income by 2015. The table at Annexure shows that for a number of countries belonging to LDCs it may not be possible to come out of low equilibrium trap. It has been also projected in UNCTAD Report on LDCs—2000 that in respect of very important social indicators such as life expectancy, under five infant mortality rate, in the level of education and gender-gap, the LDCs will be left behind by 2015.

It has been observed through the poverty alleviation experience of selected developing countries that the reduction in poverty to a very great extent was induced by the high rate of economic growth. In case of LDCs, on the basis of trends of economic growth 1980s and 1990s, the prospect for growth-induced poverty reduction appears to be very limited. During 1990-1998, real GDP per capita in the LDCs. grew only at 0.9 per cent per annum as against 3.6 per cent per annum growth in per capita income of other developing countries. Even though the nineties witnessed divergences in growth experience of the LDCs., for major group of countries belonging to this category, i.e., African LDCs, the trend towards stagnation continued.

The poverty-profile of the "poorest of the poor" poses a number of challenges in terms of policy-initiatives both at national and international level. Among the issues that calls for urgent attention by the international community is to arrest the trend towards dehumanizing poverty among the LDCs. It is a matter of great concern for the international community that over the years, several developing countries in East Asia, Latin America, South Asia have been able to reduce the degree of deprivations for the poor. For most of the LDCs. specially those in the Sub-Saharan region, the sufferings in terms of deprivations of basic needs still loom large. The growing regional gaps in important social indicators which determine the degree of human poverty, is shown at Annexure III-5. A glance at widening gap between Sub-Saharan Africa and other regions in important social indicators such as life expectancy, child mortality, illiteracy etc. reflects the neglect of vital social sectors in the process of economic development. The Action Programme which was adopted by the Third United Nation Conference on the Least Developed countries in Brussels (14-20 May, 2001) noted that the needed international support to these countries has been inadequate. The Programme of Action articulated policy and measures which should be immediately taken to improve the social indicators.

The Action Programme fixed some goals and targets in two vital sectors such as education and health. In education, policy and measures to be pursued will be as follows :

(i) Ensuring that by 2015 all children, particularly girls, children in difficult circumstances and those belonging to ethnic minorities, have access to and complete, free and compulsory primary education of good quality.

(ii) Achieving 50 per cent improvement in levels of adult literacy by 2015, especially for women, and equitable access to basic and continuing education for all adults:

(iii) Eliminating gender disparities in primary and secondary education by 2005, and achieving gender equality in education by 2015, with a focus on ensuring girls' full and equal access to and achievement in basic education of good quality.

The Action Programme also identified policies to improve health, nutrition and sanitation. Towards this end, goals and targets were fixed as under :

(i) Reducing the infant mortality rate below 35 per 1,000 live births by 2015.

(ii) Reducing the under 5 mortality rate below 45 per 1,000 live births by 2015.

(iii) Reducing the maternal mortality rate by three-quarters of the current rate by 2015.
(iv) Reducing the number of undernourished people by half by the year 2015.
(v) Reducing by half by 2015 the proportion of people who are unable to reach or to afford safe drinking water.
(vi) Reducing HIV infection rates in person 15-25 years of age by 2005 in all countries, and by 25 per cent in the most affected countries.
(vii) Increasing the percentage of women receiving maternal and prenatal care by 60 per cent.
(viii) Halving malnutrition among pregnant women and among pre-school children in LDCs by 2015.
(ix) Substantially reducing infection rates from malaria, tuberculosis and other killer diseases in LDCs by the end of the decade; reducing tuberculosis (TB) deaths and prevalence of the disease by 50 per cent by 2010; and reducing the burden of disease associated with malaria by 50 per cent by 2010.
(x) Promoting child health and survival and reducing disparities between and within developed and developing countries as quickly as possible, with particular attention to eliminating the pattern of excess and preventable mortality among girl infants and children.
(xi) Improving the health and nutritional status of infants and children.
(xii) Promoting breast feeding as a child survival strategy.

To sum up, poverty-profile of the developing world reflects marked contrast in the level of poverty among the various groups of developing countries. While on the one hand some of the developing countries succeeded in eliminating poverty or reducing it, on the other end of the spectrum we find that poverty has either remained stagnant or in some cases it has increased. The Third United National Conference on LDCs held in may 2001 in Brussels as well as the United National millennium Declaration has called upon the international community to meet the policy challenges to lift over 300 million people suffering from poverty in these countries. In future, the prospect for the eradication of poverty from the LDCs will depend on the effective implementation of the Action Programme adopted in the Third United Nations conference on LDCs (May 2001) and on the fulfillment of the commitments by the member countries of United Nations made in the Declaration on poverty eradication.

The implementation of the Action Programme adopted in the third United Nations conference on LDCs (May 2001) is of vital importance for the eradication of poverty for the LDCs. The participants in the third UN Conference on LDCs had undertaken commitments to raise the level of Human and Social Development and towards that end, they outlined a number of policy measures to build human and institutional capacities and to develop social infrastructure. Annexure III-15 gives the details of these policies. The commitments Inter-Alia included action by the LDCs for facilitating universal access to basic social services for increasing budgetary allocations in favour of social infrastructure, giving adequate priority to housing and sustainable human settlements in rural areas and in urban locations with a concentration of the poor. The Action Programme also identified action by development partners to increase ODA in support of LDCs efforts towards provision of social infrastructure and social services in order to reach the UN social targets. In the action programme specific goals and targets in sectors including educations, health care etc. were fixed. The details of these targets are in corporated in Annexure III-15.

CHAPTER IV

Indian Experience in Poverty Alleviation : Priority Tasks Ahead : Employment Generation : Human and Social Development

A Survey of Indian poverty-profile shows the influence of economic growth on poverty. Since independence, the decline in poverty has followed changes in the rate of economic growth attained by Indian economy. In the early years of planned development, the average rate of growth had leveled at a rate of 3.5 per cent per annum. Population in India grew at the rate of 2.3 per cent on average during 1950 to 1970. The net improvement in per capita income was only about 1 per cent and this low rate of growth in income did not make dent in poverty in India. Poverty only started to decline after the mid-1970s when per capita income started growing at 3 per cent per annum.

In 1973-1974, a national poverty line was worked out by the Task Force appointed by the planning commission. The Task Force estimated the poverty line as monthly per capita consumption expenditure of Rs. 49 for rural areas and Rs. 57 for urban areas at the price prevailing in years. This was equivalent per capita daily in take of 2400 calories for rural areas and 2100 calories for urban areas as per the consumption pattern of 1973-1974. The poverty line is updated by using consumer price index for agriculture labour and for urban workers. In 1973-1974 the intensity of poverty in India was estimated to be 57 per cent which included both urban and rural poor. A head-count of poor persons below the poverty line was conducted by the National Sample Survey (NSS) in 1993-1994 and according to their estimate the number of poor people in India declined by one third from 57 per cent in 1973-1974 to 37 per cent in 1993-1994. The break-up of poverty is given at Annexure IV-1.

The continued high rate of economic growth during 1980s and 1990s brought out a substantial drop of nearly 10 per cent in the number of people below poverty line. The percentage of people living below the poverty line has come down to 26.10 per cent during the year 1999-2000 as compared to 36 per cent in 1992-1993. The latest estimate of the percentage of people living below poverty-line is based on the estimate by the national sample survey organization. The latest survey has revealed that the number of people below the poverty line is higher in the rural areas at 27.09 per cent as compared with 23.62 per cent in the urban area. Inspite of a significant fall in the intensity of poverty, the number of poor in India continues to remain at a very high level of 19.32 crore of the rural population and 6.70 crore of urban population. There is a very marked disparity in the decline in poverty among the various states. Among the states, Orissa, Bihar, Madhya Pradesh etc. have very high degree of intensity of poverty. On the other hand Punjab, Himachal Pradesh, Andhra Pradesh, Haryana, Gujarat, West Bengal, these states have shown lower degree of intensity of Poverty. The trend in decline in poverty since 1970s has been explained at Annexure IV-2.

The poverty - profile of various states shows that the degree of incidence of poverty is closely related with the growth of population. In Kerala, Gujarat, Punjab and Tamil Nadu the annual rate of growth of population was less than 2 per cent between 1983-1994 and accordingly annual rate of reduction in poverty was well over 2 per cent. Kerala achieved the highest reduction in the proportion of people below the poverty line during this period. It appears therefore that a lower population has a positive anti-poverty impact. The poverty -profile of states gives us a disturbing trend that five lowest income states, which include Bihar, Uttar Pradesh, Madhya Pradesh, Orissa and Rajasthan, have been very slow in poverty reduction. The divergence between the low income states and high income states in the rate of poverty reduction increased in 1990's. In fact poverty stopped falling in low income states.

The elimination of poverty in India is impeded by several factors, which include structural bottlenecks. The structure of development in Indian economy reflects very slow rate of absorption of agriculture labour in the off – farm employment. The success of East Asian countries in the elimination of poverty to a great extent was the result of fast rate of shift of labour to non-farm sector such as manufactures and tertiary sector. This was a positive outcome of economic growth in these countries and that led to declining poverty. One of the factors contributing to the persistence of poverty in India is that a majority of workers is in the category of low productivity/unproductive sectors and as a result low wages perpetuate poverty. The population growth in unproductive sector further aggravates the problem of poverty.

The other factor of crucial importance in understanding the persistence of poverty in Indian economy is that the changes in the sources of income have not influenced the sources of employment. When the East Asian countries were growing, they succeeded in achieving fast rate of reduction in poverty because the growth had impacted the transformation in employment. On the other hand in Indian economy while the composition of the income has been rapidly moving away from agriculture, the changes in the composition of employment have been very slow. With the result, agriculture still accounts for the bulk of total employment in India and even in 1993-1994 more than 70 per cent of house-hold depended on agriculture for their livelihood. The national sample survey organization had undertaken a study in 1993 of the composition of employment and according to their findings, in rural area 71 per cent employment originated in agriculture.

The composition of rural employment in India is an important element in policy options for alleviation of rural poverty. The national sample survey had made a study of the sources of income earned by the rural poor. According to NSS report No. 409 for 1993-1994, there are two broad categories of rural poor. Approximately 50 per cent of the rural poor are self-employed in agriculture. Those who are self-employed, have some physical assets from where they derive their income. The workers in other categories have no assets and work as casual labourers and they constituted 50 per cent of rural labour in 1993-94. The major cause of poverty for asset – less agriculture labour is very low wages and uncertain job. More than 50 per cent of rural poor fall under the category of most economically disadvantageous.

According to NSS Data, in 1972–1973, about 82 per cent male and 90 per cent female workers were engaged in agriculture. In 1993-1994, 76 per cent of male and 85 per cent female labour were engaged in agriculture. It is worth noting that over two decades, only 8.6 per cent shift was absorbed from agriculture through non-agriculture activities. One of the factors contributing to very slow rate of shift of labour from rural to non-rural sector has been that quality of human resources has been very poor and skill formation has lagged behind. It is worth pointing out that low priority to education has resulted in slow occupational diversification, which is a necessary condition for removal of poverty. Most of the workers are engaged in casual work at very low rates of wages and so even though they are employed, they fall below poverty-line. According to NSS statistics, between 1970s and 1990s, there is a rise in the proportion of casual workers in India. In the causal work – sector, because of seasonality of agriculture, work is only for a part of year and also wage is at subsistence level. The point of concern is that despite efforts towards rural development between 1980s and 1990s, the percentage of rural workers dependent on agriculture has declined by less than 1 per cent and the dependence on agriculture has remained at 80 per cent. Annexure IV-3 shows increasing percentage of casual worker in rural work-force in 1993-1994, the percentage of casual labour both in the category of male and female increased as compared with 1993. The large scale under employment and unemployment have been the main factors leading to casualisation of labour. The fact that these workers have neither skill nor assets, forces them to accept casual work for their livelihood.

In order to achieve elimination of poverty from India, we need a development - strategy which can create income among the poor in order to facilitate their escape from the infliction of poverty. As is well known, the people below the poverty line have to depend only on one asset and, i.e., their labour. Unless, therefore their labour is utilized through the generation of employment opportunities, the task of lifting these poor people above the line of poverty cannot be fulfilled. The creation of employment is key to the alleviation of poverty in India. The choice of policy for an attack on poverty will be by and large determined by the prospects of creating employment.

The employment scenario in India presents some disturbing trends which limit the impact of economic growth in creating job opportunities. According to the Report of The Task Force, appointed by planning commission on Employment Opportunities (June 2001), there has been an increase in the rate of unemployment in 1998-2000 as compared with 1993-1994. There has been also a decline in the rate of growth of employment opportunities. The rate of growth in employment has declined sharply from 2.04 per cent per year during the period 1983-1984 to 0.98 per cent per year in the period 1993-1994 to 1999-2000. The sectoral pattern of the decline is alarming because the entire decline was due to slower growth in agriculture employment. It may be mentioned that agriculture still accounts for a major share of employment, i.e., 60 per cent of the labour force. Not only that the declining employment in agriculture dims the prospect for the generation of jobs in rural sector, a large part of employment generated in the rural economy provides very low income which is not sufficient to cross the line of poverty. In other words the fact that a person is employed does not necessarily mean that he has escaped poverty. Annexure IV-4 explains declining employment – opportunities in both public and private sectors.

Against the backdrop of these trends, the Report of the Task Force on Employment Opportunities has also pointed out decline in the elasticity of employment. Since labour is an input into production, an increase in output is normally associated with an increase in employment. Along with economic growth, it is normally expected that employment should be positive. In a growing economy however in a situation when growth results in increase in productivity, employment may increase proportionally less than the output. Increased productivity under these circumstances may not result in positive employment – elasticity.

In 1990s, the employment elasticity for the economy has been declining. Between 1977-1978 to 1983, the elasticity of employment was 0.53 per cent which declined to 0.15 per cent in 1999-2000. During the period 1993-1994 to 1999-2000, the sector including agriculture, community, social and personal services, which account for 70 per cent of total employment did not experience any growth in terms of employment. In other words employment elasticity in agriculture was zero during 1993-1994 to 1999-2000. In manufacturing sector also the possibility of further reduction in employment elasticity cannot be ruled out in view of ongoing process of technological modernisation and industrial restructuring.

While working out the strategy to fight poverty, the recent trends in employment need to be kept in view. As has been pointed out, the sector which at present gives maximum employment to the poor. Agriculture has shown very low rate of elasticity in employment. The services – sector has acquired dominant role in creating new employment – opportunities. It has been projected that over 70 per cent of increase in employment will come from services during next decade. The additional employment opportunities created in services sector may not absorb the unskilled rural manpower and that calls for special employment programmes which can ensure direct and targeted creation of job opportunities. The employment scenario clearly shows that economic growth by itself may not result in the creation of employment opportunities which can wipe out – poverty from India. The estimate of employment elasticity in various sectors is given at Annexure IV-5. In agriculture sector which employs approximately 70 per cent of Indian labour force, the employment elasticity has been constantly declining and between 1993-1994–1999-2000, it has been projected at zero. Annexure IV-6 gives the trends in employment growth and the rate of growth in employment in agriculture which is negative. According to projection of employment at Annexure IV-6 only service sector has the potential to add to the job-reservoir. The impact of increase in employment in service sector on poverty reduction remains uncertain because of mismatch between the requirements and supply of unskilled rural labour. These trends in the employment further necessitate anti-poverty policies to be focused on direct employment-creation schemes.

India has launched special programmes to supplement the employment generated by economic growth. These programmes are targeted to provide wage employment or self-employment to specific target groups which comprise of poor in urban and rural areas. These special programmes also include wage and self-employment programmes which are not targeted. The major ongoing employment programmes for the rural poor include Employment Assurance Programme (EAS), which is a wage employment programme, the Swaran Jayanti Gram Swarojgar Yojana (SJGSY), which is a self-employment programme and the Jawahar Gram Samridhi Yojana (JGSY). (Please see notes on to three)

The Employment Assurance Scheme was launched in 1993 and was designed to provide wage employment to unskilled rural poor who are below to poverty line. The Jawahar Gram Samridhi Yojana (JGSY) was introduced on 1.4.1999 and was designed as a programme for the direct employment generation through the construction of various types of durable assets in the rural areas. The total employment generated by these two programmes in 1998-1999 was equivalent to 4.4 million man years. Compared to the size of total rural labour force of over 300 million this is only 1.5 per cent of the total rural labour force.

For direct employment creation for the people below poverty line, the government had also launched self employment scheme which was called Integrated Rural Development Programme (IRDP). This scheme was launched in 1980-1981. Under this scheme, people below poverty line were identified and were given capital subsidy and credit from banks to set up projects. On 1.4.99, self employment programme under IRDP was merged with Swaran Jayanti Gram Sworajgar Yojana (SJGSY). There were other allied programmes related to IRDP such as Training of Rural Youth for Self Employment (TRYSEM), Million Wells Scheme (MWS). These programmes were also merged with SGSY.

In Urban area for urban poor, several programmes for the creation of wage and self-employment have been launched. The Urban Wage Employment Programme (UWEP) aims at giving wage employment to people below poverty-line. There are also schemes for self-employment for educated youth. The programme youth. The programme is called Self Employment for Educated Youth (SEEY). Later this programmes was merged with Prime Minister's Rozgar Yojana (PMRY). In 1994-1995, the PMRY. Programme was extended to cover rural areas also. The programme aimed at setting up 7 lakhs micro enterprises duing 8th plan period (1992-97). The Government's strategy to promote employment in rural areas also includes support for Khadi and Village Industries. The Rural Employment Generation Programme (REGP) of Khadi and Village Industries was launched in 8th plan. It was initially targeted to create 2 million jobs in the 8th plan period.

In order to lift the poor above poverty line, special targeted employment programmes which have been briefly described above, have a very important role in the context of Indian Policy for the eradication of poverty. Because of lack of skill, communication and education, the poor may not be able to participate in the employment opportunities created by economic growth in manufacture and service sector. The employment growth in agriculture which employs approximately 70 per cent of labour force, has been almost negligible or zero. For poverty alleviation therefore direct creation of employment is an indispensable channel through which India can succeed in the task of poverty alleviation. The success of India's Anti-poverty policy will to a great extent depend on the success of these special programmes in absorbing the vast number of poor people and thereby in raising the level of income. Special employment programmes also contribute to provide safety – nets to the poor in critical situation such as economic crisis, natural calamities etc. It is well known that poor people are most vulnerable to financial and economic crisis and to natural calamities such as flood, drought etc. These calamities increase the intensity of poverty for the poor and through the safety-nets provided by special employment programmes, the vulnerability of the poor to these disasters can be reduced.

In a market economy, it is the market which distributes access to the employment opportunities created by economic growth and the poor may not be able to take advantages of the increasing job opportunities. In the absence of linkages between the poor and the employment opportunities, the expanding job market can lead to either tightening of the market or increasing the real wages of skilled manpower. The problem of poverty is therefore, not redressed unless suitable public policy is framed for targeted employment creation.

Indian strategy for the eradication of poverty needs to refocus the targeted employment programmes which can reach poor and raise their level of income. For the programmes to succeed in reducing poverty, we have to undertake extensive research in the working of these programme so that deficiencies in the implementation of these programmes can be identified and suitably remedied. In past, several evaluations of these programmes were conducted by the Planning Commission and by other concerned authorities and organizations. It was found out that in one of major schemes for the generation of self employment in rural areas, viz, IRDP, the number of families assisted, declined from around 3.7 million per year in seventh plan to 2.2 million in the eight plan and further to 1.8 million per year in the first two years of ninth plan. Similarly in case of wage employment programmes in urban areas, it was observed that in giving employment, it covered less than one tenth of the 1 per cent of the urban labour force during 1999-2000. Through these evaluations, it was also observed that in spite of increasing expenditure on these programmes, the incremental employment was not significant. The total expenditure on the major programmes for wage employment and self employment in rural and urban areas increased sharply from Rs. 4121.33 crores in 1990-1991 to Rs. 8077 crores in 1999-2000. One of the factors that contributed to the limited impact of special employment programmes on the generation of jobs was that the desired degree of labour – intensity in the implementation of projects was not observed. The application of appropriate technology in the projects under special employment programmes constitutes a very important area of research to improve the effectiveness of employment programmes. The other areas of research include adequacy of investment, methodology of targeting, administrative bottlenecks faced in the implementation of programmes etc. It is disturbing to note that recently there has been a decline in the number of jobs generated by special employment schemes. The total number of jobs created by these programmes was 6 million in 1993-1994 and this declined to 4.4 million in 1998-1999. As pointed out earlier, in the eradication of poverty in India, the special employment programmes because of its directness and target-effectiveness and because of its high degree of labour intensity, have a special role to play.

In the Report of the Task Force on Employment Opportunities, it has been argued that quantitatively higher rate of economic growth can create more additional jobs than special employment progammes. According to projections in the report GDP growth at 8 per cent will generate an extra 14.45 million employment opportunities by the year 2012 and if the growth rate accelerates to 9 per cent per annum, this will yield an additional employment of 12.92 million by 2012. These projections are made on the assumption that the additional investment will have positive employment elasticity. These assumptions may not come through in view of the recent trends towards the declining employment elasticity experienced by the economy during 1990s. It appears therefore that special employment programmes will continue to have its importance in the generation of job opportunities and in the eradication of poverty in India.

The fulfillment of basic needs for the poor through social and human development is an important dimension of India's poverty – profile. It has been widely recognized that by raising income alone poverty cannot be removed. Poverty inflicts sufferings of various kinds on the poor in terms of lack of access to basic needs such as access to health care, education, safe drinking water, sanitation, housing etc. The deprivation of these basic facilities has been conceptualized as human poverty and for the formulation of anti – poverty policy, this forms an integral part in the choice public policy. For the formulation of appropriate policies towards the fulfillment of basic needs, certain social indicators are used by the policy – makers. These social indicators measure the degree of human poverty in a society.

In recognition of the importance of the fulfillment of basic needs for the elimination of poverty, India launched Minimum Needs Programme (MNP) in the fifth five year plan in the 1970s. Initially this included elementary education, health, water supply, roads, electricity, housing and nutrition. Later in sixth and seventh five year plans, adult education, rural sanitation and public distribution system were also added to this list. The Minimum Needs Programme (MNP) was given a new shape in

1996 and seven basic minimum services were identified. These included (i) 100 per cent coverage in primary health facilities (ii) safe drinking water to all (iii) universalisation of primary education (iv) housing to shelterless (v) nutrition support to children (vi) connectivity; rural roads to all unconnected villages and (vii) revamping of public distribution system.

The social indicators in the specific areas such as child mortality, literacy, sanitation, drinking water, housing and access to public distribution system, indicate the degree of achievement of India in the fulfillment of these basic needs. As per the estimates of national sample survey (NSSO) the overall percentage of literacy has increased from 52.2 per cent in 1991 to 62 per cent in 1997 and to 63.1 per cent in 1998. The male literacy rate has reached 74.5 per cent and the female literacy rate has improved to 51.4 per cent by 1998. In this sector, the point for concern is that there is a large gap between the rate of literacy in the urban area and in the rural area. It has been estimated that the rural literacy rate is a still at 56.7 per cent as compared with 80.1 per cent of literacy rate achieved in the urban area. In the field of education the commitment is for total eradication of illiteracy. In 1998-1999, the gross enrollment ratio for primary school children was 92.14 per cent. The ratio for upper primary stage was a still very low at 58 per cent. Please see Annexure IV-7. In the upper primary stage, the progress in enrollment is still behind the targets.

Although India has raised literacy rates, comparatively the rise has been modest one. In case of China for example by 1981, literacy rate rose to 96 per cent for male and 85 per cent for females in the age group of 15 to 90 years. China has virtually eliminated illiteracy. Similarly, Indonesia achieved 85 per cent literacy rate and Sri Lanka achieved 90 per cent literacy rate.

The other important sector which needs to be accorded priority while designing anti-poverty policy is health care. The lack of education and health care aggravates the degree of deprivations and deepens the pangs of poverty. In almost all social indicators the progress in health care is reflected. For example life expectancy at birth has doubled from 32 years in 1951 to 62.4 years in 1996. Please see Annexure IV-8 and IV-9. Similarly the infant mortality rate declined from 146 per thousand in 1961 to 72 per thousand in 1996. In realm of basic facilities also India has made considerable progress. For example in the provision of safe drinking water coverage has increased from 56 per cent in 1985 to 98 per cent in 1999 in the rural sector and from 73 per cent in urban sector to 90 per cent during the same period.

The access to water supply and sanitation is an important index of achievement in health sector. Availability of drinking water and the provision of sanitation facilities are the basic minimum requirements for healthy living. According to an estimate by the ministries of rural development and urban development there has been a significant progress in supply of drinking water between 1985 and 1999. It has been estimated that in 1999, the coverage in the rural area for drinking water was 98 per cent and in the urban area it was about 90 per cent. In the field of sanitation however the progress has been very slow and by 1999 approximately 50 per cent of the population was covered by sanitation facilities. Please see Annexure IV-10.

In comparative terms however Indian achievement in health sector has been rather limited. The national average of infant mortality rate at 80 is still higher than many other Asian countries. Similarly life expectancy at birth is well below that of China, Sri Lanka, and other East Asian countries. It has been also estimated that approximately 63 per cent of the children under 5 years of age in India suffer from mal-nutrition. The comparative performance of India and some East Asian Countries is at Annexure IV-11.

As in education so in health care system there is a distinct urban bias and also there is a gender-gap. It has been estimated that the expenditure in rural area per capita in health services is much less than in urban area. It may be also be pointed out that total Indian government expenditure on health is just 1.3 per cent of GDP and covers only 22 per cent of total expenditure. It is worth noting that no country can secure sustainable poverty reduction without healthy and well educated population. While economic development creates the demand for human resources of high quality and facilitates development of infrastructure, social development results in supply of better quality and more productive human resources. Therefore one of the policy challenges for poverty reduction in India is to adequately develop its health care system and education.

Raising the level of social and human development, has been one of the thrust areas in the choice of policy for the elimination of poverty in India. The basic needs of life by and large comprise of education, health, sanitation, water supply facilities and social security. The provision of these basic needs has to be necessarily by the state because the investments in these sectors do not yield returns to provide sufficient incentive to the private enterprise. Indian development strategy has recognized these imperatives in the formation of public policy and have taken several initiatives to meet the basic needs of the poor.

Plan and Non-Plan expenditure of the Central Government on various social sector services increased from a level of Rs. 9608 crore in 1992-1993 to Rs. 36270 crore in 2000-01 (BE); an increase of about four times in eight years. As a ratio to total expenditure, the combined plan and non plan expenditure of the Centre rose from 8.1 per cent in 1992-1993 to 10.7 per cent in 2000-2001. Expressed as a ratio to GDP at current market prices, the expenditure on social services of central government increased from 1.28 per cent in 1992-1993 to 1.66 per cent in 2000-2001. Please see Annexure IV-12.

As a percentage to the GDP at current market prices, plan expenditure of the Centre on major schemes of social sectors has been in the range of 1.1 per cent to 1.2 per cent during the last decade. However, significant increases in central plan outlay is observed in education, especially elementary education, health, women and child development, and family welfare programmes in the budgeted estimates of 2000-01. The central plan outlay in 2000-01 (BE) as compared to the previous year's revised estimate increased by 24.3 per cent for education and 26.5 per cent for elementary education programmes; by 29.8 per cent for health sector programmes; by 16.8 per cent for women and child development; and by 12.8 per cent for family welfare schemes.

In the fulfillment of basic needs, the social indicators in almost all sectors such as education, health etc. have improved in India. While there has been over-all improvement in the social indicators, some imbalances in the fulfillment of basic needs have also emerged in the process. These imbalances include gender-gaps, urban-rural gaps and wide variation in the improvement in the social indicators of various states. The overall percentage of literacy has increased from 52.2 per cent in 1991 to 62 per cent in 1997 as per NSSO estimates and 63.1 per cent in 1998. According to National Family Health Survey (NFHS) 1998-1999. While male literacy rate has touched 74.5 per cent, the female literacy rate even after improvement was 51.4 per cent by 1998. The urban literacy rate has increased to 80.1 per cent though the rural literacy rate was still low at 56.7 per cent in 1998. Please see Annexure IV-13.

The gross enrollment ratio (GER) was 92.14 per cent in 1998-1999 for primary school children and it was 58 per cent for upper primary stage. It was observed that the proportion of girls enrolled both for primary and upper primary levels was lower than the gross enrollment of boys. In health sector also these gaps have surfaced. Please see Annexure IV-7.

In India, the life expectancy at birth for females has increased from 44.7 years in 1971 to 60.9 years in 1994. The increase has been faster than that of men. The life expectancy at birth for women in India, however, was lower than that for men until 1981. In 1991, life expectancy at birth of women surpassed that of men.

There are large differences in female health attainment across states in India. Life expectancy at birth varied widely between 53.8 years in Madhya Pradesh and 74.7 years in Kerala during 1989-1993. Similarly, female infant mortality rate was a low of 12.9 in Kerala and a high of 98.1 in Orissa in 1997, while in the same year, the maternal mortality rate per 100,000 live births varied between 29 in Gujarat and 707 in Uttar Pradesh. Please see Annexure IV-14.

The Infant Mortality Rate (IMR) and Child Mortality Rate (CMR) declined during the 1980s and 1990s, but are still very high in comparison with many other developing countries. In 1997, both the IMR and CMR for girls were higher than for boys by about 2 per 1000. MMR of 408, which translates to one maternal death in every 200 pregnancies, paints a disturbing picture of maternal health care.

Because of the persistence of gender-gap in the social and human development, women have not been able to participate in the socio-economic changes that India is witnessing. In the formulation of social sector development policies, it has been recognized that women should be empowered economically and socially to become a strong force in the development of the country. Several policy initiatives towards this direction have been taken by the government. These include Rural Women's Development and Empowerment Project (RWDEP), Rashtriya Mahila Kosh, Balika Samridhi Yojana (BSY) Indira Mahila Yojana (IMY) etc. Rural Women's Development and Empowerment Project (RWDEP) came into operation in 1998. The objective of this project is empowerment of women through participation and income-generation. This project has been now renamed as Swasakti. Rashtriya Mahila Kosh (RMK) was created in 1993 to meet the Micro needs of poor and assets-less women in the informal sector. Since its formation, it has given credit worth Rs. 77.36 crore to benefit 350 thousand women. Indira Mahila Yojana (IMY) aims at empowerment of women and was launched in 1995-96. Balika Samridhi Yojana (BSY) was launched in 1997 and its objective is to change the attitude towards girl-child. To ensure that projects for the empowerment of women are not constrained by lack of finance, the government introduced the Women's Components Plan (WCP) in 9th plan. It monitors the funds made available by ministries and departments such as health, labour, agriculture, rural development etc, for the benefit of women.

In important areas such as employment, literacy it is necessary that urgent measures are taken to arrest the trend towards emerging gender-gap. Women account for very low share in the labour force and, i.e., only 29 per cent of the total labour force in the country. Similarly their literacy rate at 39 per cent very poorly compares with male literacy rate at 64 per cent in 1991.

Human and social development in India is characterized by wide variations in the social indicators among individual states. Annexure IV-14 shows the performance of states in improving social indicators such as infant mortality rate (IMR) literacy, life expectancy rate etc. It will be observed from Annexure IV-14 that infant mortality rate (IMR) is very high in Orissa, Madhya Pradesh, as compared with Kerala, Tamil Nadu and Punjab where it is very low. Similarly Kerala, Karnataka and Tamil Nadu achieved much higher rate of life expectancy at birth in comparison to U.P., Bihar, Madhya Pradesh and Orissa. The other area of wide disparity is literacy. In the attainment of literacy rate, literacy at 93 per cent of Kerala is much higher than compared to Bihar, Madhya Pradesh, Orissa, Rajasthan and Uttar Pradesh. There are wide variations in the attainment of female health across states. In case of female, life expectancy at birth varied widely between 53.8 years in Madhya Pradesh and 74.7 years in Kerala during 1989-1993. Similarly, female infant mortality rate was 12.9 in Kerala and 98.1 in Orissa in 1997. The maternal mortality rate per hundred thousand life birth varied between 29 in Gujarat and 707 in Uttar Pradesh? Please see Annexure IV-14.

Kerala's success in increasing employment and reduction in poverty has been closely associated with very high level of social and human development. In a major study on poverty, Datt and Ravalliom (1996), pointed out that Kerala brought about rapid reduction in poverty through human development. The rate of reduction in poverty during 1957-1958 to 1990-1991 was highest in Kerala among all Indian States.High level of human development enabled Kerala to exploit overseas employment opportunities and thereby raising the level of income of their people. Between 1961-1962 and 1993-1994, rural and urban poverty as measured by the headcount declined by 65.57 per cent in Kerala as against 40.85 per cent reduction in poverty in India as a whole.

One of the salient features of reduction of poverty in Kerala was that in spite of the fact that average per capita growth in income in Kerala during last four decades was half of the level of all India GDP growth, Kerala made remarkable progress in the reduction in poverty. It was choice of appropriate public policies that enabled Kerala to achieve high level of human development and employment for its labour – force. The level of human development achieved by Kerala can be compared to some of the developing.

The comparative performance of states in improving social indicators and in the reduction of incidence of poverty establishes a close relationships between social progress and its positive impact on the elimination of poverty in the developing world. Education can be a very powerful factor in reducing poverty. In case of China for example rising literacy rate greatly impacted poverty reduction.

Kerala achieved life expectancy of 72 years, male literacy rate of 93.62 per cent and a female literacy of 89.91 per cent. As will be observed from the Annexure IV-14, this rate of achievement in human and social development compares very closely with Republic of Korea, Malaysia,Indonesia who succeeded in attaining very high level of social indicators.

To sum up, Indian policy framework to eliminate poverty is characterized by a multi-faceted strategy. Acceleration in the rate of economic growth in 1980s and 1990s, positively impacted the eradication of poverty in India. In spite of reduction in poverty, there are about 260 million persons estimated to be below the line of poverty. Their income has to be raised at a level that will lift them up above the line of poverty. Economic growth by itself is a long term remedy for poverty. Even if Indian economy registers expected rate of economic growth between 8 to 9 per cent during tenth five years plan, this can not guarantee the income creating effects of economic growth among the poor. Therefore, rapid generation of employment opportunities which can reach poor through targeted programmes, has to be a priority objectives to effectively address the problem of income poverty.

The other dimension of poverty is human poverty. It has been observed that while India has achieved significant improvement in social indicators, the level of social and human development needs to be raised in order to reduce the degree of human deprivations and to increase the capabilities of the poor. India still lags behind many developing countries in meeting basic needs of the poor such as education, health, sanitation, drinking water etc. Human and Social Development in India also suffers from several imbalances which include state-disparities in social indicators, emerging gender gap, urban-rural gap in the attainment of social and human development. These imbalances will need to be corrected through new policy initiatives both by the states and by the centre. Our analysis has shown that the low level of social development attained by some states cannot be just explained in terms of low income. The experience of poverty alleviation in various states has shown that the choice of policy is of crucial importance in reducing human poverty.

Poor remains most vulnerable to natural calamities. India, frequently faced natural calamities such as flood, drought etc. The poor remains most vulnerable to these calamities as they depend on agriculture for their livelihood. These calamities increase the number of poor and also intensify the sufferings of those who are already poor. The problem of poverty in Indian context cannot be solved unless massive investments are made to control flood and to ensure adequate irrigation to avoid droughts.

Notes

1. Jawahar Gram Samridhi Yojana

The other important policy initiative in fighting poverty, taken by the Indian Government was the launching of Jawahar Gram Samridhi Yojana (JGSY). This was launched w.e.f. 1.4.1999 by the restructuring of Jawahar Rojgar Yojana. The JGSY was the creation of demand driven community village infrastructure, which could increase opportunities for sustained employment. The implementation of the JGSY will be entirely by the village Panchayat. One of the important features of JGSY is that 22.5 per cent of JGSY funds have been earmarked for individual beneficiary schemes for Scheduled Castes and Scheduled Tribes. As regards the works to be taken up, all works that result in the creation of productive community assets can be taken up by village Panchayat according to felt needs of the people. In the choice of projects, it has been envisaged that priority should be given to infrastructure for Scheduled Castes and Scheduled Tribes habitators, community infrastructure for education and health. The performance of JGSY is given at Annexure from IV-15 to IV-19.

2. Employment Assurance Scheme

The driving principle of the anti-poverty strategy of India has been the recognition that the efficient use of available human resources is the most effective way of alleviating poverty. Accordingly, in development strategy, emphasis was laid on mechanism through which employment—opportunities for target-groups could be increased. Towards this direction, the Employment Assurance Scheme (EAS) was launched on 2nd October 1993, in 1778 identified blocks of 257 districts situated in the drought prone areas, desert areas, tribal areas etc. This was restructured w.e.f. 1.4.1999 and is at present a single wage-employment programme. The Zilla Parshads have been designated as the implementing authority. The primary objective of the EAS is the creation of the additional wage employment opportunities. The secondary objective is to create durable assets for employment. EAS is open to rural poor living below poverty line. A maximum of two adults per family will be provided wage-employment. The funds are shared between the centre and states in the ratio of 75:25 while providing employment, preference is given to Scheduled Castes/Scheduled Tribes. The performance of EAS is given of Annexures from IV-20 to IV-24.

3. Swaranjayanti Gram Swarojgar Yojana

In its recent anti poverty strategy the government of India has brought to focus alleviation of poverty in the rural areas and has taken several innovative measures to fight poverty in rural area. A new self-employment programme namely Swaranjayanti Gram Swarojgar Yojana (SGSY) has been launched from 1.4.1999. The SGSY came into being after restructuring of earlier programme which included Integrated Rural Development Programme (IRDP), Development of Women and Children in Rural Areas (DWCRA). Million Wells Schemes (MWS), Training of Rural Youth for Self-Employment (TRYSEM), etc. The evaluation of these programmes brought out some limitation of these programmes. One of the deficiencies of these programmes was that these programmes could not work in a coordinated way and income to rural poor could not be generated on a sustainable basis. The objective of the restructuring was to make the programme more effective in providing a sustainable income throught micro enterprise development.

The SGSY covers all aspects of self-employment by organising rural poor into self-help groups, infrastructure—build up, credit—facility, technology and by establishing micro-enterprises. The objective of SGSY is to bring assisted family above poverty line in three years. The SGSY focusses on group-approach. This involves organisation of poor into self-help groups and their capacity-building. SGSY also provides credit and subsidy to the assisted families known as Swarojgaris and lays emphasis on skill—development through training courses. SGSY also helps in upgrading technology in identified activities. Below the poverty line families in rural areas constitute the target-group of the SGSY. Within the target group, special safe-guard has been provided to vulnerable societies. The Scheduled Castes/ Scheduled Tribes would account for at least 50 per cent of the Swarojgaris, women for at least 40 per cent and disabled at least 3 per cent. A comprehensive system of monitoring has been adopted under SGSY. The implementation of the programme is monitored by Central and State Government and also by District rural Development Agencies. The SGSY is financed as 75.25 are sharing basis between the centre and the states.

The SGSY is of recent origin and since 1999 April, it has made some progress in the implementation of its various programmes to assist poor people in the rural areas. The performance of SGSY is given of Annexure from IV-25 to IV-29.

CHAPTER V

An Attack on Poverty : Responding to Globalisation and Emerging Challenges

Globalisation can be defined as a process which reduces barriers to International transactions involving trade, finance, investments, technology etc. The effect of globalisation is to integrate markets for goods, services, capital, and technology across the countries. The process of globalisation can be projected through statistics of trade, flow of capital, investment and also by degree of market-integration. More than one-fifth of global output was exported in 1990s which is double the proportion of export in 1950s. Total world merchandise trade increased from about 23 per cent of global GDP in 1960 to about 39 per cent of GDP in 1999. The spectacular growth in international trade was stimulated by post-war reduction in tariff and non-tariff barriers, reduction in the cost of transportation and communication and by expanding size of market. The share of developing countries in global trade has also increased from 23 to 29 per cent.

The process of globalisation has influenced the course of economic development. Increasing international trade alongwith changing pattern and composition of trade has brought a number of developing countries into the global production network and has created new opportunities for economic growth. A very important technological dimension of globalisation has been increasing Intra-firm trade among multinational corporations. This accounts for one third of world trade at present. The current revolution in technology has increased the scope for the industry to subdivide the process of production and distribution into various parts that can be the relocated anywhere in the world according to comparative advantages. The outsourcing is done through sub-contracting, joint ventures and by direct investments by multinational corporations in developing countries. Major break-through in communication system such as utilisation of satellites, cables, internet has shrunk both space and time and has enabled the multinational firms to organize their production and distribution in an integrated fashion across the globe.

In the process of globalisation the developing countries have new potential for industrialisation and development. Through global production networks, the transnational firms procure their supplies from firms in the developing countries. The production of components in the developing countries has increased the participation of these countries in the international trade and production system. One of the salient features of globalisation has been that the old international division of labour based on the core-periphery relations has been replaced by new division of labour in which the cost-effective labour is procured from across the globe. Industry has outstripped agriculture as a source of economic growth in the developing world. The shift in the structure of GDP of developing countries has stimulated the process of increasing trade between the developing and the industrialised countries which is based not on the old division of labour but on comparative advantages in manufactures. In other words globalisation has added dynamism to the growth of developing countries through international trade. The development - experience of China and of Newly Industrialized economies (Asian NIES) and of some other economies such as Indonesia, Thailand, Taiwan, show-cases the contribution that globalisation can make to accelerating economic growth in developing countries through increasing trade.

Globalisation has resulted in positive trade-outcomes for the developing countries. Their share of trade in the world trade has increased from 23 per cent in 1985 to 29 per cent in 1995. Intra-developing country trade has also increased from 31 per cent of total developing country trade in 1985 to 37 per cent in 1995. Between 1985 and 1995, the share of manufactured products in the export of developing countries increased from 47 per cent to 83 per cent. This reflects the process of internationalisation which the global economy has been going through.

The expanding international trade and foreign investment which has resulted from increasing globalisation in 1980s and 1990s has made significant contribution to raise the level of income in some developing countries where there has been wide spread poverty.

The development experience of Asian NIES (Newly Industrialised Economies) demonstrated the success that can be a achieved by taking advantage of integration with global economy through trade, finance and investment-linkages. The countries such as South Korea, Hong Kong, Singapore successfully utilized the opportunities created by globalisation and converged towards the per capita income level of advanced economies. During 1965 and 1995 the Republic of Korea for example experienced a ten fold rise in per capita income. The rapid income growth of Korea is a model of export – led economic growth which occurred in most of Asian economies between 1965 to 1980s. The increase in exports resulted in high rate of saving and investments and through foreign investment, new technology was applied in the process of industrialisation. The rapid rate of economic growth which resulted in high rate of reduction in poverty in these countries shows that the positives impact of globalisation on economic growth and reduction of poverty results from appropriate policy-response towards forces of globalisation.

In this context Chinese success in combining rapid economic growth with reducing the rate of poverty underlines the positives outcomes of globalisation on fighting poverty. Chinese foreign trade expanded at a very rapid rate after China launched on opening up trade. Between 1978 upto 1997, the total value of imports and exports increased by 14.5 times from US$20.6 billion in 1976 to US$ 325.1 billion in 1997. The average annual growth rate in trade was 15.5 per cent. China ranked 10th in the world in international trade up from 30th rank in 1978. The share of exports to GDP reached more than 20 per cent up from 5 per cent in 1979. The expanding foreign trade stimulated economic growth and China was able to reduce the intensity of poverty considerably in a short span of time.

The other important channel through which globalisation

positively impacted the development prospects of developing country was the globalisation of financial markets. In 1980s, lack of adequate finance constrained to a great extent the attainment of sustainable economic growth. The globalisation of financial markets affects development because finance plays such an important role in economic growth and industrialisation. Financial globalisation affects growth in two ways: by increasing the global supply of capital, and by promoting domestic financial development. Rapid improvements in technologies for collecting, processing, and disseminating information, along with the opening of domestic financial markets, the liberalisation of capital account transactions, and increased private saving for retirement, have stimulated financial innovation and created a multi trillion-dollar pool of internationally mobile capital.

The 1990s have seen a consistent trend toward more flexible exchange rate regimes and the liberalisation of capital account transactions. The latter involves changes in policies toward different types of private capital flows, such as foreign direct investment, foreign bond and equity investment, and short-term borrowing from abroad. The new policy-initiatives, have made many developing countries a more attractive destination for foreign investment which include macroeconomic stabilisation and structural reforms, privatisation policies, relaxed rules on foreign direct investment. Rising confidence in the economic prospects of developing countries in the 1990s was reflected in the fact that foreign direct investment accounted for greater proportion of capital inflows, which indicated a commitment to invest over a longer time horizon than portfolio investments like equity holdings.

By 1997 approximately half of capital inflows to developing countries was foreign direct investments. The developing countries have also participated in the process of globalisation of finance. In 1996 they invested 51 billion dollars abroad. The share of developing countries in global FDI was 15 per cent in 1996.

Foreign Direct Investment (FDI) has registered maximum increase among various kinds of capital inflows. Out of about 2000 billion dollars of net capital inflow in developing countries during 1990-98 more than dollars 700 billion was in form of foreign Direct Investment. It may be recalled here that in 1980s the much needed Foreign Direct Investment lagged behind and the average annual growth of these inflows in developing countries did not exceed 15 per cent. In 1990s, the rate of annual growth in the FDI in the developing countries rose to 28 per cent. Annual out-flows of Foreign direct Investments have grown more than six fold between 1983 and 1990 and has continued to grow more than double the flow of trade in 1990s. The developing countries increased the share of FDI from 16 per cent of the total FDI in the second half of the 1980s to 28 per cent in the 1990s.

The globalisation of finance has however not benefited all the developing countries. The benefits from the increase in the flow of FDI to the developing countries accrued to only a few developing countries. During 1992 to 1997, the ten leading emerging market economies accounted for more than three quarters of total FDI inflows to developing countries. China, Brazil and Mexico accounted for almost half of the total inflow. The skewed distribution of FDI to developing countries is evident from the per capita FDI in various regions. During the period 1992 to 1997, per capita FDI in Sub-Saharan Africa was under dollar 5 a year, compared with dollar 62 in Latin America and dollar 31 in ASEAN. Country-wise also, the flow of FDI reflects a very uneven distribution. Per capita FDI in Uganda, during 1992 to 1997 and in Ghana was dollar 3 and dollar 6 respectively, during this period, in China, per capita FDI was dollar 21, dollar 35 in Brazil, dollar 79 in Mexico and dollar 223 in Malaysia. There were several factors which contributed to the widening gap in FDI flows among regions and countries. These included growing attractiveness for fast growing developing countries in East Asia, China and the openess of these economies. This trend in FDI, spelt out the limitations of globalisation. In a globalising economy, the countries which are trapped in low level of economic growth, are deprived of the benefits of globalisation. This trend also underlines the fact that globalisation will fail to address the problem of poverty and economic growth unless the various imbalances in trade and investments which create new opportunities for economic growth, are removed.

There are certain other aspects of globalisation, which may adversely effect the link between economic growth and poverty-alleviation. The implementation of new technologies has increased structural unemployment and especially in the developing countries, it is bringing out economic hardship to some section of society. The source of competitive advantages has also changed as an off-shoot of globalisation. The countries who possess resources for innovations, gain competitive advantages on those countries who have limited resources for undertaking technological innovation. The role of innovations in stimulating economic growth has increased. The Schumpeterian cycle of products moves fast during era of globalisation and renders products and technologies obsolete. For example, in telecommunication industry, copper cables have been replaced by fiber optics and by satellites systems. Similarly revolution in information technology has replaced mechanical machine by computer network. These innovations are introduced by industrially advanced countries who can pay for the research and development. The introduction of innovation in the production cycle enables the rich country to retain competitive edge. The other development which adds to the competitive advantage of industrially advanced country is the change in the origin of wealth. The source of wealth is moving from physical capital and raw materials per worker to human skills and knowledge. Wealth creation in the 21st century will depend especially on the ability to access increasing knowledge and to make productive use of expanding stock of knowledge and information. The rate of economic growth in future with depend on the relative capacity of a nation to access knowledge and information.

The challenge of globalisation is to enable the developing countries to participate in the creation of wealth that has occurred as a result of globalisation. In a situation when the source of wealth is moving from traditional factors of production to knowledge and information technology, it is imperative that through resource transfer, developing countries should be equipped with new sources of wealth.

The effects of globalisation on poverty have been widely debated. According to some economists, globalisation through increasing global integration is expected to bring about convergence. In other words income-inequalities between countries will diminish as the economies of the poor countries grow more rapidly than those of the developed countries.

Rising income in the developing world will enable these countries to wipe-out poverty and hence globalisation enhances prospects for reduction in poverty. There is also a theoretical base for this perspective on globalisation. According to development-theory, the rates of return to capital will diminish along the path of the economic growth in the developed countries as it becomes more abundant relative to labour. As capital in a developing economy is a scarce factor of production, its rate of return should exceed the rate of return of capital in the advanced countries. In the absence of barriers to capital-mobility, which the globalisation facilitates, capital will flow from developed economies to developing economies and will raise economic growth. Eventually this will close income-gap between developed and developing countries.

The empirical evidence however has not supported the optimism on the results of globalisation in closing the gap between the high-income and low-income countries. There has been very limited convergence between developing and developed countries. The countries in East Asia and some other developing countries showed tremendous capacity to integrate with the global economy and they also registered rapid rate of economic growth. On the other hand, a number of developing countries could not attain required level of economic growth and hence they witnessed a trend towards divergence rather than towards convergence. For those countries who have not been able to converge with the developed countries, the prospect of removing poverty will be limited. The assumption that the rate of return on capital in the developing countries will be higher than that of developed countries, has not proved to be valid in all cases. Only those developing countries who could capture technological innovations and who had skilled manpower and could attract large scale investment and could expand their trade, could reap the benefits of higher return on capital. The pattern of per capita income growth of the developing countries, raises questions regarding the benefits of globalisation. Since a number of developing countries have not been able to register rapid economic growth, they were also unable to make a dent in the poverty.

Globalisation has resulted in expanding international trade. But for developing countries as a whole, the growth of export has lagged behind the growth of imports and most of the developing countries suffered imbalances in their trade and some non-fuel primary commodities exporters continue to suffer decline in their terms of trade inspite of expanding trade. Globalisation can not yield optimum results unless imbalances in the trade sector are corrected. There are a number of other imbalances that the world economy suffers from, in addition to the imbalances in international trade. The persistence of widespread poverty and underdevelopment in the global economy results in structural impediments for the developing countries and as a consequence they are not able to fully participate in the process of globalisation. The persistence of human deprivations in several parts of Asia, Africa and Latin America shows that globalisation has failed to offer poor countries and the poor parts of the population adequate opportunities for development. While Globalisation has resulted in gains to some developing countries in terms of faster economic growth, it is debatable whether it has resulted in adequately addressing the problem of poverty-alleviation.

The utilisation of technology is an important channel through which developing countries can succeed in achieving rapid economic growth and alleviating poverty. The development experience of 90's has clearly demonstrated that not many developing countries have the capacity and mechanism to acquire necessary technology for economic development. It has been established that the concentration of poverty has been more marked in those developing economies where the rate of economic growth has been low. The challenge of globalisation therefore is how to link these low-income countries with the forces of globalisation.

The incidence of poverty in Africa is closely related to the region's low level of national income. Sub-Saharan Africa has the largest proportion of people living on less than US dollar one a day which is the international poverty line drawn by the World Bank to quantify the magnitude of poverty in developing countries. This region has remained at a low level of income since 1970s and real income in most of the countries in the region have remained stagnant. Growth in per capita income averaged 1.5 per cent in the 1960s, 0.8 per cent in the 1970s and minus 1.2 per cent in 1980s. Between 1987 and 1994 these countries suffered from further decline in income.

It appears that globalisation has bypassed the economy of Sub-Saharan Africa. While the globalisation has brought about wave of trade liberalisation and multifold increase in the flow of foreign capital to various regions of the developing world, it has not benefited Sub-Saharan Africa. They have not shared trade-benefits resulting from globalisation which accrued to other developing countries. Instead they suffered annual trade losses. The result of all these imbalances, has been that Sub-Saharan Africa has witnessed a very slow rate of decline in poverty and in some countries in the region, the number of poor has increased.

Most of the countries in Africa, whose rate of economic growth has been very slow, face acute scarcity of capital to finance critically minimum investment in their economies. There has been multifold expansion of foreign direct investment (FDI) and of portfolio finance. Even though there has been rapid globalisation of capital markets, the Least Developed Countries (LDC) have not been able to tap these resources. The 1990s have also witnessed a trend towards slowing of Official Development Assistance and of lending by multilateral financial institutions. ODA, has been the corner-stone of international cooperation for development and it can be directly addressed to the anti-poverty programmes as compared with financial flows in the capital market. ODA has the potential to help the developing countries in their fight against poverty. However, it is a matter of great concern that since 1992, the flow of ODA to the developing countries has declined. The ratio of aggregate ODA of OECD member countries to their GNP has come down.

The efforts of developing countries to alleviate poverty have been greatly impeded by their increasing indebtedness. Even though there has been enormous increase in the flow of foreign capital across the globe, some of the developing countries suffer from increasing size of external debt. Debt-servicing absorbs large portion of financial resources and of export-receipts of these countries and therefore they continue to be in low-income equilibrium-trap. The other important imbalance that the global economy suffers is from widening gap in education and skill between the developing and the developed countries. Even though globalisation has opened new opportunities for increasing production and income, the developing countries suffer from limitations in their capacity to utilize these opportunities. Lack of skills, and inadequate basic education do not allow the poor in the developing countries to participate in the growth-process unleashed by globalisation. It is a well known fact that globalisation has led to a knowledge-based economy. Thus, new economy operates to the advantage of those who have knowledge and it operates against those who do not have knowledge. One of the fall-outs of the process of rapid Globalisation in 1990s has been the birth of "knowledge-based" production. Even within a country those who lack knowledge will not be able to participate in these developments and both at the level of country and at the level of individual, marginalisation will continue along with the forces of globalisation.

Globalisation has some indirect effects on the income-distribution within a society. One of the off-shoots of globalisation is that over a period of time, wages of unskilled workers fall and the demand for skilled workers increases. This trend results from the shifts that the technology makes in the frontiers of production. This shift of labour takes place also from agriculture and other sectors to high-value added manufacturing sectors and to service-sector. This raises the wage-level of technical manpower and the task of raising income of the poor becomes more complex and difficult.

As globalisation reaches more nations, there emerges disparities in the capacity of national economies to capture the benefits of globalisation. For those countries who have low savings-base and are not able to attract foreign capital, the benefits from openness of trade will be limited. Structural bottlenecks in production coupled with low level of savings inhibit many developing countries from reaping gains from open trade.

In a globalising economy, It is through foreign capital and the technology that it infuses in production that gives competitive edge to national economies. The globalisation has created and integrated capital-market on a global scale. This limits the choice of policy makers effectively implementing policies for stabilisation for growth. For example, if government wants to stimulate growth by lowering interest rate domestic capital will move abroad to seek higher rates of return. Similarly if government wants to stimulate growth by increasing expenditure, imports will increase in a free economy. In a situation when local manufacture does not increase, the developing economy will not have the benefit of creating employment opportunities in the economy. If it depreciates currency to reduce trade-deficit, it will reduce domestic business and will also adversely affect equity capital.

Globalisation has rendered conventional trade theory redundant. According to conventional trade theory, free trade increases demands for the products from the countries with relatively abundant factor while it reduces demands for relatively scarce factor. In developing economies, unskilled labour is an abundant factor and skilled labour is scarce factor. According to conventional trade theory, through free trade the wage-gap between skilled and unskilled worker will eventually narrow down because of increasing demand for unskilled workers in a developing economy.

In the 1960s, East Asian countries enjoyed comparative advantage in the production of labour-intensive products and were able to absorb unskilled manpower. This led to poverty-alleviation along with the process of economic growth. Recent technological progress is generally labour-replacing and is biased towards specific skill and knowledge-uses. The spread of technology in global market raises the demand for skilled and better-trained labour and thus globalisation bypasses the large work-force who are unskilled and work in the back-water sectors. Openness to trade, forces firms to move into high value and sophisticated consumer products, the production of which requires use of labour with varying degrees of skill-intensity. In today's globally linked production net-work, unskilled workers have very limited scope for utilisation. The multinational companies produce goods, which cater to the sophisticated market and hence they require skilled workers. The other factor for increasing the demand for skilled workers is that the goods produced by the subsidiary plants of multinationals are largely re-exported to competitive markets. Yet another factor that adversely affects the prospects of poor unskilled workers is that they are located in the subsistence rural economy and in traditional sector where multinational corporations generally do not invest. They prefer areas where there is a well-developed infrastructure and skilled labour is available, global manufacturers seek new technologies which tend to be labour - saving and which raises demand for skilled workers at the expense of on unskilled ones. This leads to wage-disparities between skilled and unskilled workers and also increases the income-gap in the society. Globalisation also affects the distribution of income in a developing economy. Globalisation leads to the rise in profit-income relative to wage earnings. Global integration also affects the distribution of wage earnings among the various categories of workers.

While global economic inter-dependence offers prospects of higher productivity and higher income, it also closely links national economies to exogenous financial developments. The financial crises of 1997-99 has put the growing interdependence among countries in the spotlight and has led to their scrutiny. International capital flows to developing countries, though still concentrated in a dozen or so host economies, are rapidly becoming a major force, making its regulation difficult.

In an integrated global capital-market, short-term speculation in currency trading takes place and the capital is also created by speculative activities. In such a situation the capital that is created through speculative trading, makes national economies vulnerable to global forces. It can create financial instability in a developing economy. The Mexico crisis of 1994 and the recent East Asian crisis of 1997 has shown how integrated developing countries loose control over the movement of foreign capital.

The financial crisis that the East Asian countries suffered in 1997, was to a great extent caused by the uncontrolled wave of globalisation. Most of the investment in theses countries was financed by credit-expansion and through financial inflows. This led to high debt to equity ratio. Many financial institutions and firms borrowed heavily because of the interest-rate-differential. These loans were short-term and were invested in projects with a very long gestation period. The other factor was that these funds were also invested in real estate development, which had uncertain pay-off. Massive capital-inflows were facilitated by the liberalisation of the capital-account and by deregulation of the domestic financial market which, the globalisation brought about. Once the crisis triggered, capital-outflows started and it led to currency depreciation, stock market collapse, liquidity shortage and finally to the cooling of domestic demand.

The crisis also adversely affected the spectacular progress made by the countries in reducing poverty . The increase in the rate of unemployment in the affected countries was one of the social consequences of Asian financial Crisis of 1997, which had directly impacted the poverty-profile of these countries. There was collapse in the demand for labour, which was caused by retrenchment and bankruptcies. In the Republic of Korea, one of the affected countries, the unemployment rate increased from 2.3 per cent in October 1997 to 8.2 per cent in November 1998. The rate of unemployment also doubled in Thailand, Malaysia from 1997 to 1998. In Indonesia, the rate of unemployment varied between 15 to 20 per cent by the end of the 1998.

The crisis unfolded problems of protecting the poor in this situation. The limited social security and welfare system of the affected countries could do little to shield people against drastic fall in their living conditions. While crisis affects both poor and the rich, it is the poor and the more vulnerable segments of the society, which are less well prepared and have fewer means to cope with impoverishment.

Globalisation is an irreversible process. During last three decades, it has stimulated economic growth and has created additional wealth. The empirical evidence of development – experience has amply shown that for the eradication of poverty from the developing world, sustained economic growth in all regions of the developing world is an indispensable pre-requisite. The prospect for poverty reduction will depend on the extent to which globalisation will positively impact growth in the developing world. The benefits of globalisation have not accrued to all developing countries. In some regions of the developing world the persistence of high intensity of income and human poverty presents serious challenges for the choice of policies for the national governments as well as for the international community.

The globalisation has created new opportunities for the developing countries such as the revolution in information technology and globalisation of finance and trade. The revolution in information technology has the potential to help the developing countries leapfrog barriers to development by linking them to the global economy and by improving their access to knowledge. The internet and mobile telephones offer new opportunities for the developing countries to improve the infrastructure to attract foreign investment. At present the developing countries are constrained in realizing these advantages because of digital divide. In most of the developing countries, the telecommunication sector has not fully evolved which can facilitate access to Internets.

Through rapidly increasing globalisation of finance, the constraint imposed by the external resources gap can be removed. Foreign Direct Investment (FDI) to developing countries has increased from US$ 36 billion in 1992 to US$ 155 billion in 1999, more them three time the level of Development Aid. What is needed is to create conditions for directing the flow of foreign investment to those developing countries and especially to the Least Developed Countries (LDCs) where the resources are needed most. Globalisation can benefit the developing countries only when the economic and technological links are created between the developed and the developing countries. The poverty-alleviation experience of the successful developing countries in East Asia underlined the contribution that foreign direct investment can make to reduction in poverty. If developing countries are not able to access increasing foreign capital, there is possibility that globalisation can bypass these countries.

The other important channel through which globalisation can impact the creation of income and reduction in poverty is through expanding international trade. Some of the developing countries such as LDCs have not being able to take advantages of expanding trade. In international trade there are some other areas which call for new policy initiatives to enable developing countries to participate in the expanding international trade. Developed countries still maintain tariff and non-tariff barriers against the exports of developing countries in the sectors which include agriculture, textile etc. It is necessary that in future trade negotiations in WTO, priority should be given to the multilateral liberalisation of agriculture. At present developing countries also face non-tarif barriers in their access to the markets of developed countries because of European Union's common agriculture policy.

While the process of globalisation has speeded up in 1980s, the pattern of economic growth in the developing countries has also witnessed a trend towards polarisation of these countries between high and low income clusters. For the developing countries in the low income clusters, globalisation has led to marginalisation for some developing countries especially developing countries in Africa. The income gap has widened in these countries. The per capita income level of Developing Countries in Africa fell from 14 per cent of the industrial country level in 1965 to just 7 per cent in 1995. On the other hand, the four Asian NIES, increased their per capita income level from 18 per cent of the industrial country level in 1965 to 65 per cent in 1995. The stagnation in economic growth for some developing countries has created pockets of poverty and that presents a challenge to the international community for the eradication of poverty.

As will be observed from the above analysis, it is not easy to assess the impact of globalisation on economic development and reduction of poverty. Globalisation has its downsides which have been explained in details in this chapter. One of the most disturbing features of globalisation has been the marginalization of a number of developing countries in the developing world. Most of the developing countries who have not be able to participate in the process of globalisation, are trapped in low income equilibrium trap. The current debate on globalisation has led to the recognition of the urgent need to manage globalisation in a way that adds momentum to economic development in these economies and also reverses trend towards marginalisation. In this context, there have been two important initiatives on the part of international community which deserve special mention to illustrate the challenges that globalisation is faced with. The United Nations Millenium Summit—September 2000 in its declaration annexed at Annexure V-1 recognised the limitation of globalisation. The declaration in following paragraph summed up the challenges faced by the globalisation.

"We believe that the central challenge we face today is to

ensure that globalisation becomes a positive force for all the world's people. For while globalisation offers great opportunities, at present its benefits are very unevenly shared, while its costs are unevenly distributed. We recognized that developing countries and countries with economies in transition face special difficulties in responding to this central challenge. Thus, only through broad and sustained efforts to create a shared future, based upon our common humanity in all its diversity, can globalisation be made fully inclusive and equitable. These efforts must include policies and measures, at the global level, which correspond to the needs of developing countries and economies in transition, and are formulated and implemented with their effective participation."

The Declaration "Inter Alia" included important policy initiatives to accelerate the rate of economic growth in developing economies so as to enable them to reap the dividends of globalisation. These special measures are listed at Annexure V-1.

The other important initiative in this direction taken by the international community weas the adoption of an Action programme in the Third UN conference on LDCs (2001). The Action Programme included identification of policies and measures which if taken by the international community and by the National Governments, could mitigate the negative fall-outs of globalisation on the low income economies. The relevant extracts from the Action Programme which outline these policies, are as Annexed as V-2. The prospect of the reduction of poverty in globalising economy to great extent will depend on the progress in the implementation of these policies.

Epilogue

The choice of policy for the eradication of poverty has been very widely debated among the economists and the policy-makers. One of the areas in which the debates have intensified, relates to the effectiveness of economic growth in addressing the problem of poverty. There is a school of thought who believes that if an economy is growing, poverty will be declining through the process of "trickle-down". According to this school, to eradicate poverty in a developing economy what is required is to accelerate the rate of economic growth.

The empirical evidence has suggested that the goal of elimination of poverty with its multi-dimensional characteristics cannot be achieved without the support of public policy. Income is only one dimension of poverty and the other dimension is the provision of basic needs. It is the fulfillment of basic needs that creates suitable conditions for increasing the capabilities of the poor. As the case-studies in Chapter II have shown that a country can attain a high level of social and human development even with a relatively lower per capita income. In other words it is the choice of policy that determines the success of a country in the eradication of poverty, which reflects both lack of income and lack of human capabilities.

It has been seen in the past that even with comparatively low income, a country can meet the basic needs of its population more effectively. Sri Lanka achieved a high rate of reduction in human poverty even though its attainment in terms of per capita income was very modest in comparative terms. The life-expectancy rate of 69 years achieved by Sri Lanka and infant mortality rate of 37 per one thousand life-births compares very closely with those levels which were attained by industrially advanced countries who attended very high level of economic growth.

The eradication of poverty cannot be left to economic growth because the fulfillment of basic needs cannot wait for trickle-down effects of economic growth. The lack of basic needs such as health care, lack of safe drinking water, lack of sanitation, lack of education etc. adversely affect the capability of poor. The provision of basic needs cannot be left to market because where the motivation is profitability, the service cannot be provided at affordable rates which the poor can pay. In the fulfillment of basic needs such as health-care, state has to intervene because the investment in these sectors may not be attractive. Sri Lanka again provides a show-case were the choice of public policy raised the capabilities of the poor by ensuring good health. In specific terms the Malaria-eradication programme of Sri Lanka as early as 1946 and 1947, resulted in lower death rate and a high rate of life expectancy for its people. The education programme of Sri Lanka is also an example of priority to social development given in public policy. In Sri Lanka, adult-literacy increased from 38 per cent in 1946 to 78 per cent in 1971. In India, Kerala, has set an example in attaining high level of social and human development for its people as compared to India as a whole. For example, Kerala had achieved 72 per cent literacy as compared to Indian average of 39 per cent in 1978. In health sector also achievement of Kerala underlines the importance of choice of policy in the eradication of poverty. In 1978, infant mortality rate in Kerala was 39 as compared with all India average of 126. In these cases it is very clearly demonstrated that for the fulfillment of basic needs, the slow and indirect impact of economic growth may not be effective.

The fight against poverty has to be both at national and international level. Prospect for rapid reduction in poverty in the developing world to a great extent will depend on the growth-prospects of these countries. It has been estimated that sustained growth of per capita income of 3 per cent per annum will be the minimum necessary rate of economic growth for eradicating poverty substantially. It may be pointed that in 1999 a number of developing countries could not achieve this rate of economic growth in per capita terms. It is also projected that for a number of developing countries it may not be possible to achieve 3 per cent per capita income-growth in near future. It is unlikely therefore that in the short-term there will be a major dent in poverty through economic growth. In Africa for example the GDP is expected to increase by 4 per cent in 2001 and this will give per capita GDP of one and half per cent per year. This may not be sufficient for the elimination of poverty for most of the developing countries in Africa.

The poverty-profile of South Asia as well as of Africa present challenges, which call for new policy-initiatives both at national and international level. The emerging trends in global economy will influence the degree of success of developing countries in their fight against poverty. In the beginning of 21st century, global perspectives have changed. A combination of new economic variables have affected the foundations for future development. In the USA and in the other industrially advanced countries, recent years have witnessed a strong output growth with low inflation and with low rate of unemployment. Inflation and business cycles, which used to be de-stabilising factors in the global economy, have significantly weakened. The global economy has been strengthened by strong economic performance of the USA over nearly a decade and by the evolving new economy which rapid forces of globalisation and of integration in the world economy have created.

The question is that to what extent the new forces in the global economy can have favorable effects on the elimination of widespread poverty in the developing world. It will depend to a large extent on the prospect that the new economy provides for developing countries to share the benefits that it has created. There have been several factors such as improved communication, declining transport costs, trade liberalisation and global integration which can be expected to contribute towards the economic development of developing countries and thereby creating new prospects for the eradication of poverty. As we have seen in the earlier chapters that globalisation has its pitfalls and through market forces alone developing countries may not be able to share the benefits of global economic integration and from technological innovations. Globalisation is also one of the factors which contribute to growing inequality among nations at international level and also domestically within nations.

The prospect for making an effective dent in poverty depends to a great extent on the policy-framework to counter the negative aspects of globalisation and to create conditions to enable the developing countries to share the benefits from globalisation and from revolution in information and communications technology. The developing countries will need resources to fight poverty and that calls for international cooperation. There is a positive development in this regard. Global consensus on the elimination of poverty has built-up and recently a number of initiatives have been taken at national and international level to effectively combat poverty.

Annexures

ANNEXURE I-1

U.N. Millennium Declaration-Development and Poverty-Eradication

We will spare no effort to free our fellow men, women and children from the object and dehumanizing conditions of extreme poverty, to which more than a billion of them are currently subjected. We are committed to making the right to development a reality for everyone and to freeing the entire human race from want.

We resolve therefore to create an environment-at the national and global levels alike-which is conducive to development and to the elimination of poverty.

Success in meeting these objectives depends, inter alia, on good governance within each country. It also depends on good governance at the international level and on transparency in the financial, monetary and trading systems. We are committed to an open, equitable, rule-based, predictable and non-discriminatory multilateral trading and financial system.

We are concerned about the obstacles developing countries face in mobilising the resources needed to finance their sustained development. We will therefore make every effort to ensure the success of the High-level international and intergovernmental Even on financing for Development, to be held in 2001.

We also undertake to address the special needs of the least developed countries. In this context, we welcome the Third United Nations Conference on the Least Developed Countries to be held in May 2001 and will endeavour to ensure its success. We call on the industrialsed countries.

To adopt, preferably by the time of that conference, a policy of duty-and quota-free access for essentially all exports from the least developed countries.

To implement the enhanced programme of debt relief for the heavily indebted poor countries without further delay and to agree to cancel all official bilateral debts of those countries in return for their making demonstrable commitments to poverty reduction; and

To grant more generous development assistance, especially to countries that are genuinely making an effort to apply their resources to poverty reduction.

We are also determined to deal comprehensively and effectively with the debt problems of low-and middle-income developing countries, through various national and international measures designed to make their debt sustainable in the long term.

We also resolve to address the special needs of small island developing States, by implementing the Barbados Programme of Actions and the outcome of the twenty-second special session of the General Assembly rapidly and in full. We urge the international community to ensure that, in the development of a vulnerability index, the special needs of small island developing States are taken into account.

We recognise the special needs and problems of the landlocked developing countries, and urge both bilateral and multilateral donors to increase financial and technical assistance to this group of countries to meet their special development needs and to help them overcome the impediments of geography by improving their transit transport systems.

We Resolve Further

To halve, by the year 2015, the proportion of the world's people whose income is less than one dollar a day and the proportion of people who suffer from hunger and, by the same date, to halve the proportion of people who are unable to reach or to afford safe drinking water.

To ensure that, by the same date, children everywhere, boys and girls alike, will be able to complete a full course of primary schooling and that girls and boys will have equal access to all levels of education.

By the same date, to have reduced maternal mortality by three quarters, and under-five child mortality by two thirds, of their current rates.

To have, by then, halted, and begun to reverse, the spread of HIV/AIDS, the scourge of malaria and other major diseases that afflict humanity.

To provide special assistance to children orphaned by HIV/AIDS.

By 2020, to have achieved a significant improvement in the lives of at least 100 million slum dwellers as proposed in the "Cities Without Slums" initiative.

We Also Resolve

To promote gender equality and the empowerment of women as effective ways to combat poverty, hunger and disease and to stimulate development that is truly sustainable.

To develop and implement strategies that give young people everywhere a real chance to find decent and productive work.

To encourage the pharmaceutical industry to make essential drugs more widely available and affordable by all who need them in developing countries.

To develop strong partnerships with the private sector and with civil society organisations in pursuit of development and poverty eradication.

To ensure that the benefits of new technologies, especially information and communication technologies, in conformity with recommendations contained in the ECOSOC 2000 Ministerial Declaration, are available to all.

ANNEXURE I-2

Human Needs: Global Targets and Timetables

- By the year 2000, universal access to basic education and completion of primary education by at least 80 percent of primary school-age children; closing the gender gap in primary and secondary education in all countries before the year 2015.
- By the year 2000, life expectancy of not less that 60 years in any country.
- By the year 2000, reduction of mortality rates of infants and children under five years of age by one-third of the 1990 level, or 50 to 70 per 1,000 live births, whichever is less; by the year 2015, achievement of an infant mortality rate below 35 per 1,000 live births and an under-five mortality rate below 45 per 1,000.
- By the year 2000, a reduction in maternal mortality by one-half of the 1990 level; by the year 2015, a further reduction by one-half.
- Achieving food security by ensuring a safe and nutritionally adequate food supply, at both the national and international levels a reasonable degree of stability in the supply of food as well as physical, social, and economic access to enough food for all, while reaffirming that food should not be used as a tool for political pressure.
- By the year 2000, a reduction of severe and moderate malnutrition among children under five years of age by half of the 1990 level
- By the year 2000, attainment by all peoples of the world of a level of health that will permit them to lead a socially and economically productive life, and to this end, ensuring primary health care for all.
- Making accessible through the primary health-care system reproductive health to all individuals of appropriate ages as soon as possible and no later than the year 2015, in accordance with the Programe of Action of the International Conference of Population and Development, and taking into account the reservations and declarations made at that Conference, especially those concerning the need for parental guidance and parental responsibility

- Strengthening efforts and increasing commitments with the aim, by the year 2000, of reducing malaria mortality and morbidity by at least 20 per cent compared to 1995 levels.
- By the year 2000, eradicating, eliminating, or controlling major diseases constituting global health problems, in accordance with paragraph 6.12 of Agenda 21.
- Reducing the adult illiteracy rate-the appropriate age group to be determined in each country-to at least half its 1990 level, with an emphasis on female literacy; achieving universal access to quality education, with particular priority being given to primary and technical education and job training, combating illiteracy, and eliminating gender disparities in access to, retention in, and support for education.
- Providing, on a sustainable basis, access to safe drinking water in sufficient quantities, and proper sanitation for all.
- Improving the availability of affordable and adequate shelter for all, in accordance with the Global Strategy for Shelter to the Year 2000.
- Monitoring the implementation of those commitments at the highest appropriate level and considering the possibility of expediting their implementation through the dissemination of sufficient and accurate statistical data and appropriate indicators.

ANNEXURE II-1

Africa Lags behind and the Gap is Widening

	Infant mortality (per 000 live births)			*Primary Enrollment (net)*			*Income poverty (Absolute no. below poverty line, (millions)*		
	1980	*1997*	*Change*	*1980*	*1997*	*Change*	*1987*	*1998*	*Change*
Sub-Saharan Africa	115	91	-26	78	77	-1	217	291	74
East Asia and Caribbean	56	37	-51	111	118	6	415	278	-137
Latin America and Caribbean	60	32	-88	105	113	7	64	78	14
Middle East and North Africa	95	49	-94	87	96	9	25	21	-4
South Asia	119	77	-55	73	100	27	474	522	48

Source : World Bank, World Development Indicators.

ANNEXURE III-1
List of Least Developed Countries (LDCs)

1. Afghanistan
2. Angola
3. Bangladesh
4. Benin
5. Bhutan
6. Burkina Faso
7. Burundi
8. Cambodia
9. Cape Verde
10. Central African Republic
11. Chad
12. Comoros
13. Democratic Republic of the Congo
14. Djibouti
15. Equatorial Guinea
16. Eritrea
17. Ethiopia
18. Gambia
19. Guinea
20. Guinea Bissau
21. Haiti
22. Kiribati
23. Lao People's Democratic Republic
24. Lesotho
25. Liberia
26. Madagascar
27. Malawi
28. Maldives
29. Mali
30. Mauritania
31. Mozambique
32. Myanmar
33. Nepal
34. Niger
35. Rwanda
36. Samoa
37. Sao Tome and Principe
38. Senegal
39. Sierra Leone
40. Solomon Islands
41. Somalia
42. Sudan
43. Togo
44. Tuvalu
45. Uganda
46. United Republic of Tanzania
47. Vanuatu
48. Yemen and Zambia

ANNEXURE III-2
Incidence of Poverty in Selected Least Developed Countries (LDCs)

Countries	*Survey Year*	*Percentage of Population Below $1 a Day*[a]	*With per Capita Income Below $2 a Day*[a]
Bangladesh	1996	29.1	77.8
Burkina Faso	1994	61.2	85.8
Central African Republic	1993	66.6	84.0
Ethiopia	1995	31.3	76.4
Gambia	1992	53.7	84.0
Lesotho	1993	43.1	65.7
Madagascar	1993	60.2	88.8
Mali	1994	72.8	90.6
Mauritania	1995	3.8	22.1
Mozambique	1996	37.9	78.4
Nepal	1995	37.7	82.5
Niger	1995	61.4	85.3
Rwanda	1983-1985	35.7	84.6
Sierra Leone	1989	57.0	74.5
Uganda	1992	36.7	77.2
United Republic of Tanzania	1993	19.9	59.7
Yemen	1998	5.1	35.5
Zambia	1996	72.6	91.7
Average LDCs[b]		**43.7**	**74.7**
Average 55 other DCs[b]		**13.1**	**34.6**

The Least Developed Countries 2000 Report.

ANNEXURE III-3
Selected Economic and Social indicators for the LDCs and other DCs

A Economics Indicators	*Year / Period*	*LDCs*	*Other DCs*
GNP per capita, PPP	1980	724	2 587
(Current international dollars)	1990	1179	4 078
	1997	1343	4 598
Share of labour in agriculture (%)	1990	75	32
Share of agriculture in GDP (%)	1997	34	17
Share of primary commodities	1980	86.3	76.6
In total merchandise exports (%)	1997	68.9	31.9
Export concentration index	1997	0.553	0378
Export instability index	1980-1997	20.3	13.4
Energy consumption (kg coal eq. Per capita) : Coal, oil, gas and electricity	1980	64	508
	1996	69	898
Feulwood and charcoal	1980	212	125
	1996	210	135
Annual population growth (%)	1960-1970	2.4	2.3
	1990-1997	2.6	1.7
Age dependency ratio	1975	0.93	0.88
(dependents to working-age population)	1998	0.87	0.68

The Least Developed Countries 2000 Report.

ANNEXURE III-4
LDCs Real GDP and Per Capita GDP Growth Rates, 1980-1990 Vs 1990-1998 (Per cent)

	GDP growth rates		*Per capita GDP growth*	
	1980-1990	*1990-1998*	*1980-1990*	*1990-1998*
Least Developed countries of which	2.5	3.2	-0.1	0.9
LDCs excluding Bangladesh	1.9	2.4	-0.9	0.4
African LDCs	1.6	2.1	-1.1	-0.4
Asian LDCs	4.3	4.7	1.7	2.9
Island LDCs	4.8	3.5	2.2	0.9
Memo items :				
World	3.1	2.5	1.4	1.1
Low income countries	6.3	7.1	4.3	5.4
Low and middle income countries	3.3	3.4	1.4	1.9
DCs (excluding LDCs)	3.9	5.2	1.9	3.6
Mean of growth rates in :				
LDCs	2.7	3.0	0.4	0.5
DCs (excluding LDCs)	3.0	3.9	0.8	2.0
T-test for the difference between the means	-1.5	-5.3*	-2.4*	-9.1*

The Least Developed Countries 2000 Report

ANNEXURE III-5
Africa Lags Behind and the Gap is Widening

	Infant mortality (per 000 live births)			*Primary Enrollment (net)*			*Income poverty (Absolute No. below poverty line, millions)*		
	1980	*1997*	*Change*	*1980*	*1997*	*Change*	*1987*	*1998*	*Change*
Sub-Saharan Africa	115	91	-26	78	77	-1	217	291	74
East Asia and Caribbean	56	37	-51	111	118	6	415	278	-137
Latin America and Caribbean	60	32	-88	105	113	7	64	78	14
Middle East and North Africa	95	49	-94	87	96	9	25	21	-4
South Asia	119	77	-55	73	100	27	474	522	48

Source : World Bank, World Development Indicators.

ANNEXURE III-6

Annual Average Growth of Primary Commodity Prices of Direct Relevance to the LDCs (Per cent)

	1989-1993	*1994-1997*	*1998*	*1999*
Total	-3.8	6.0	-13.0	-14.2
All food	-2.8	7.3	-14.3	-18.3
Food	-1.7	4.8	-13.8	-18.1
Tropical beverages	-8.2	23.3	-17.3	-20.9
Coffee	-10.8	31.3	-28.5	-23.2
Tea	1.9	4.9	4.3	-0.7
Agriculture raw materials	-1.3	2.6	-10.8	-10.3
Tobacco	3.1	7.6	-5.5	-7.0
Cotton	-0.6	10.4	-8.3	-22.9
Jute	-1.5	5.8	-14.2	-2.0
Ores and metals	-7.4	5.6	-16.5	-1.8
Copper	-5.6	6.3	-27.3	-4.9
Crude Petroleum	4.2	5.0	-31.8	7.6

The Least Developed Countries 2000 Report.

ANNEXURE III-7

External Resource Gap as Share of Investment, Government Expenditure, Government Consumption Expenditure and GDP in the LDCs and other DCs, 1980-1998

	African LDCs	*Asian LDCs*	*Island LDCs*	*LDC average*	*Other DCs*
Percentage of Gross Domestic Investment					
1980-85	99.3	55.8	117.6	101.8	27.8
1985-90	85.5	53.6	123.6	94.6	16.5
1990-95	93.5	44.4	133.0	92.5	21.2
1995-98	82.7	41.7	124.7	79.3	22.5
Percentage of total Government expenditure					
1980-85	70.5	75.4	121.2	86.2	24.5
1985.90	57.6	52.3	111.1	75.2	14.0
1990-95	72.2	43.3	67.5	75.1	19.7
1995-98	61.9	43.6	84.0	62.0	21.4
Percentage of Government consumption expenditure					
1980-85	104.4	118.9	146.7	116.7	41.1
1985-90	101.1	101.5	144.8	113.4	22.6
1990-95	109.2	85.2	193.1	119.4	32.8
1995-98	117.4	89.7	211.5	123.0	37.6
Percentage of GDP					
1980-85	17.1	13.0	42.7	21.6	6.9
1985-90	14.9	10.2	42.7	19.6	3.7
1990-95	17.5	9.9	48.7	19.9	5.0
1995-98	17.2	10.8	42.1	18.1	5.5

The Least Developed Countries 2000 Report

ANNEXURE III-8

LDCs : Long-term Net Capital Inflow by Type of Flow, and Aggregate Net Transfers, 1988-1998 (in million dollars)

	1988	1989	1990	1991	1992	1993	1994	1995	1996	1997	1998
Official net resource	12100	11978	13388	14214	14157	13563	13124	12253	11760	11145	10403
Aggregate net resource flows	10850	11025	12607	12283	12290	11285	12138	11193	9969	9078	9054
Grantsa	6207	6276	8322	8886	8683	7992	9140	8725	6674	6379	6984
Other official flows	4643	4749	4285	3396	3607	3293	2998	2469	3295	2698	2070
Private net resource flows	1249	953	782	1931	1867	2278	986	1061	1791	2067	1274
Net FDI	279	517	83	1799	1460	1748	849	1078	1809	1425	1593
Portfolio equity flows	—	—	—	—	—	—	77	49	40	8	27
Net private debt flows	970	436	699	132	407	530	60	-67	-58	634	-345
Interest payment, total	1693	1567	1492	1565	1145	1260	1265	1705	1399	1431	1452
Profit remittances on FDI	405	516	675	583	668	684	708	723	674	739	773
Aggregate net transfers	10504	10323	11653	12451	12645	11894	11394	10432	9867	9182	8376

The Least Developed Countries 2000 Report

ANNEXURE III-9

Debt Service Payments and Social Sector Expenditures in Selected LDCs, 1995-2002

	United Republic of Tanzania		*Mauritania*		*Mali*	
	1995/96-1997/98	*2000/01-2002/03*	*1997-98*	*2000-02*	*1995-97*	*2000-01*
Total social sector	213.4	—	77.5	109.4	125.8	215.0
Expenditure ($ millions) of which :						
Health	60.8	—	17.9	24.2	48.3	81.0
Education	152.5	—	53.1	60.5	77.4	135.0
Total debt service paid	160.1	146.5	89.4	82.3	74.4	93.4
per cent of total social sector expenditure	75	—	114	75	59	43.0
Total debt service due	480.5	146.5	142.9	82.3	139.5	93.4
Per cent of total social sector expenditure	225	—	184.4	75	111	43.0

The Least Developed Countries 2000 Report

ANNEXURE III-10
Progress of the LDCs in Meeting Selected International Development Goals

	Infant Mortality (per 1,000 live births)					Net primary school enrolment (per cent)				
	Actual trajectory		Required trajectory[a]			Actual trajectory		Required trajectory[b]		
	1990	1998	1990	1998	2015	1990	1997	1990	1997	2015
	(1)	(2)	(3)	(4)	(5)	(6)	(7)	(8)	(9)	(10)
Afghanistan	164.0	149.2	164.0	129.0	54.7	25.0	49.7	25.0	46.0	100
Angola	130.2	123.6	130.2	102.4	43.4	45.4	34.7	45.4	60.7	100
Bangladesh	90.6	72.8	90.6	71.2	30.2	64.0	75.1	64.0	74.1	100
Benin	104.4	86.7	104.4	82.1	34.8	45.9	67.6	45.9	61.0	100
Bhutan	..	60.9	..	..	..	..	..	..	..	100
Burkina Faso	105.4	104.0	105.4	82.9	35.1	27.0	32.3	27.0	47.4	100
Burundi	118.8	118.2	118.8	93.5	39.6	54.0	35.6	54.0	66.9	100
Cambodia	121.6	101.6	121.6	95.7	40.5	99.9	99.9	99.9	99.9	100
Cape Verde	65.0	54.7	65.0	51.1	21.7	99.9	99.9	99.3	99.5	100
Central African Republic	102.2	98.4	102.2	80.4	34.1	53.2	46.2	53.2	66.3	100
Chad	118.0	98.9	118.0	92.8	39.3	40.8	47.9	40.8	57.4	100
Comoros	84.0	62.9	84.0	66.1	28.0	53.1	50.1	53.1	66.2	100
Dem. Rep. of the Congo	95.8	90.3	95.8	75.4	31.9	54.4	58.2	54.4	67.2	100

Contd.

	(1)	(2)	(3)	(4)	(5)	(6)	(7)	(8)	(9)	(10)
Djibouti	117.8	106.2	117.8	92.7	39.3	31.8	31.9	31.8	50.9	100
Equatorial Guinea	121.0	105.9	121.0	95.2	40.3	90.8	79.3	90.8	93.4	100
Eritea	81.4	60.7	81.4	64.0	27.1	..	29.3	..	..	100
Ethiopia	124.2	106.8	124.2	97.7	41.4	25.1	35.2	25.1	46.1	100
Gambia	108.6	76.4	108.6	85.4	36.2	52.5	65.9	52.5	65.8	100
Guinea	136.0	118.3	136.0	107.0	45.3	29.0	45.6	29.0	48.9	100
Guinea-Bissau	145.0	128.4	145.0	114.1	48.3	42.4	52.3	42.4	58.5	100
Haiti	85.4	70.4	85.4	67.2	28.5	..	..	..	..	100
Kiribati	65.0	58.0	65.0	51.1	21.7	..	..	..	..	100
Lao People's Democratic Rep.	108.2	95.7	108.2	85.1	36.1	65.3	73.0	65.3	57.0	100
Lesotho	101.6	93.0	101.6	79.9	33.9	73.0	68.6	73.0	80.6	100
Liberia	168.0	114.4	168.0	132.2	56.0	..	..	..	..	100
Madagascar	103.0	92.0	103.0	81.0	34.3	..	..	..	..	100
Malawi	135.4	133.8	135.4	106.5	45.1	49.7	98.5	49.7	63.8	100
Maldives	59.8	30.6	59.8	47.0	19.9	..	..	..	..	100
Mali	135.6	116.5	135.6	106.7	45.2	21.2	38.1	21.2	43.3	100
Mauritania	104.6	90.0	104.6	82.3	34.9	..	..	..	..	100
Mozambique	150.4	134.5	150.4	118.3	50.1	47.0	39.6	47.0	61.8	100
Myanmar	93.8	78.2	93.8	73.8	31.3	82.7	99.3	82.7	87.5	100

Contd.

	(1)	(2)	(3)	(4)	(5)	(6)	(7)	(8)	(9)	(10)
Nepal	101.2	77.2	101.2	79.6	33.7	80.7	78.4	80.7	86.1	100
Niger	150.0	118.0	150.0	118.0	50.0	25.1	24.4	25.1	46.1	100
Rwanda	132.4	123.1	132.4	104.2	44.1	65.9	..	65.9	75.4	100
Samoa	27.0	25.0	27.0	21.2	9.0	..	..	..	..	100
Sao Tome and Principle	60.9	48.5	60.9	47.9	20.3	..	..	..	..	100
Sierra Leone	189.0	169.0	189.0	148.7	63.0	..	..	..	..	100
Solomon Islands	29.0	22.2	29.0	22.8	9.7	..	..	..	..	100
Somalia	151.8	120.6	151.8	119.4	50.6	..	..	..	..	100
Sudan	85.4	69.1	85.4	67.2	28.5	..	..	..	..	100
Togo	81.0	78.2	81.0	63.7	27.0	75.0	82.3	75.0	82.0	100
Uganda	104.4	100.7	104.4	82.1	34.8	..	..	..	..	100
United Rep. of Tanzania	98.7	85.0	98.7	77.6	32.9	51.4	48.4	51.4	65.0	100
Vanuatu	56.2	35.5	56.2	44.2	18.7	70.7	71.3	70.7	78.9	100
Yemen	109.6	82.0	109.6	86.2	36.5	..	..	..	..	100
Zambia	107.3	113.7	107.3	84.4	35.8	83.4	72.4	83.7	88.3	100

The Least Development Countries 2000 Report .

ANNEXURE III-11

How Long will the LDCs Take to Reach $900 Per Capita Income Levels if Current Trends Persist?

Already there	*18-25 years*	*25-50 Years*	*50-100 years*	*> 100 Years*	*Negative growth or Stagnant*
Cape Verde	Bhutan	Bangladesh	Benin	Burkina Faso	Angola
Equatorial Guinea	Lao PDR	Guïnea	Cambodia	Malawi	Burundi
Maldives	Lesotho[a]	Mosambique	Eritrea	Mali	Chad
Samoa	Sudan	Uganda	Ethiopia	Yemen	Comoros
Vanuatu			Mauritania		Dem. Rep. Of the Congo
			Nepal		Gambia
					Guinea-Bissau
					Haiti
					Madagascar
					Niger
					Rwanda
					Sao Tome and Principe
					Sierra Leone
					Solomon Islands
					Togo
					United Rep. Of Tanzania
					Zambia

The Least Developed Countries 2000 Report.

ANNEXURE III-12

International Development Goals

1. The proportion of people living in extreme poverty should be reduced by at least one half by 2015.
2. There should be universal primary education in all countries by 2015.
3. Progress towards gender equality and the empowerment of women should be demonstrated by eliminating gender disparity in primary and secondary education by 2005.
4. The death rates for infants and children under the age of life years should be reduced in each developing country by two-thirds between 1990 and 2015.
5. The rate of meternal mortality should be reduced by three quarters between 1990 and 2015.
6. Access should be available through the primary health-care system to reproductive health services for all individuals of appropriate ages, no later than 2015 .
7. There should be a current national strategy for sustainable development, in the process of implementation, in every country by 2005, so as to ensure that current trends in the loss of environment resources are effectively reversed at both global and national level by 2015.

ANNEXURE III-13

Relevant Extracts from Action Programme Regarding Mobilizing Financial Resources

COMMITMENT 7: MOBILIZING FINANCIAL RESOURCES

An enabling environment with peaceful solution of conflicts and respect for internationally recognized human rights, including the right to development, provides the best context for domestic and international resource mobilization. Equally, it requires the definition of a clear and consistent set of public objectives, sound macroeconomic policies, efficient management of public revenue and expenditure, better allocation of resources and incentives to prevent capital flight and to encourage private savings and tax reforms, and a solid framework to implement or economic reform programmes.

There is an immediate need to mobilize the financial resources that are required to implement the objectives and priorities as well as the targets that are set our in this Programme of Action aimed at the sustainable development of the LDCs. However, there is very limited scope, in the foreseeable future, to meet the multiple development finance requirements of LDCs with domestic resources because of sluggish growth or economic stagnation, widespread poverty and a weak domestic corporate sector. The large investment requirements of LDCs imply a need for new and additional resources and efforts to increase ODA to LDCs supportive of national programmes of action, including poverty eradication strategies.

(A) Domestic Resource Mobilization

The key to increasing domestic resource mobilisation and reducing dependence on external finance lies in achieving a firm structural basis which would sustain high per capita growth rates.

1. Action by LDCs

(i) Taking the necessary measures to stimulate domestic savings, with the goal of increasing domestic saving rates;

(ii) Developing efficient and appropriate financial systems, including micro-finance, and an appropriate legal and regulatory framework;

(iii) Establishing stronger links between financial sector and development goals and priorities;

(iv) Promoting innovative financial mechanisms such as microcredit programmes to mobilize savings and deliver financial services to the poor, including smallholders and self-employed, particularly women, within an appropriate legal and regulatory framework;

(v) Strengthening efforts at enforcing prudential regulations governing banks and other financial institutions and providing central banks and other regulatory bodies with appropriate legal authority and supervisory and surveillance capacity to enforce compliance with relevant laws and regulations;

(vi) Continuing to improve the performance and competitiveness of both private and public sector banks through recapitalisation, expanding private participation, providing managerial training, strengthening accounting and audit practices and developing modern management information systems;

(vii) Improving the efficiency and equity of tax collection systems, and whenever possible aiming at broadening the tax base, and enhancing the effectiveness and transparency of public expenditure, bearing in mind the interests of the poor;

(viii) Enacting policies actively seeking to attract flight capital back from abroad;

(ix) Preventing corruption, bribery and money laundering, illegal transfer of funds and other illicit activities by both public and private entities.

2. *Actions by Development Partners*

(i) Supporting LDC efforts to ensure that aid and debt relief measures support rather than undermine domestic resource mobilisation efforts. This implies constant attention to the productivity and sustainability of investments financed through aid, as well as awareness of the fiscal implications of aid and debt relief;

(ii) Programming mechanism through which domestic resource mobilization in LDCs can be enhanced by making use of aid resources;

(iii) Supporting the efforts of LDCs in the areas of financial sector development and reform and in improving access of the poor to credit;

(iv) Assisting the efforts of all LDCs to strengthen institutional capacity and regulatory frameworks for preventing corruption, bribery, money laundering and illegal transfer of funds, as well as for the repatriation of those funds to the countries of origin.

(B) Aid and its Effectiveness

Despite the positive effects that domestic policies can achieve in mobilization of local resources, ODA will remain a critical resource for achieving the objectives, goals and targets of this Programme of Action. It is essential to consider fully both the quantitative and qualitative aspects of aid and the effective coordination of this aid. An essential condition for achieving this objective and reducing aid dependency in LDCs is the improvement of aid volumes and aid effectiveness. Also, increasing national ownership through better integration of external aid into macroeconomic and sectorial programmes is crucial, as are relevant auditing, accounting and management practices. National programmes of action offer possible framework for this task.

(1) Action by LDCs

LDCs will seek to :

(i) Set up, in the context of national development strategies, the necessary public sector auditing and accounting systems, coherent budgets and medium-term expenditure plans;

(ii) Integrate and coordinate aid within national plans and priorities and enhance administrative capacity;

(iii) Design, implement and regularly update national development strategies through dialogue between government and national stakeholders to enhance national policy ownership;

(iv) Identify sectors where ODA can have the most significant catalytic effect on efforts to eradicate poverty, and foster sustained economic growth and sustainable development.

(v) Establish, with the assistance of development partners, information systems to monitor the use and effectiveness of external resources, including ODA;

(vi) Support institutional arrangements that encourage public-private partnerships.

2. *Action by Development Partners*

Donor countries will implement the following actions that they committed to at the second United Nations Conference on the Least Developed Countries as soon as possible :

(i) Donor countries providing more than the 0.20 per cent of their GNP as ODA to LDCs; continue to do so and increase their efforts;

(ii) Other donor countries which have met the 0.15 per cent target; undertake to reach 0.20 per cent expeditiously;

(iii) All other donor countries which have committed themselves to the 0.15 per cent target; reaffirm their commitment and undertake either to achieve the target within the next five years or to make their best efforts to accelerate their endeavours to reach the target;

(iv) During the period of the Programme of Action, the other donor countries; exercise individual best efforts to increase their ODA to LDCs with the effect that collectively their assistance to LDCs will significantly increase;

(v) Support LDCs' efforts to develop information systems which record, at the recipient country level, indicators and other relevant information relating to aid effectiveness, both for individual donors and for the donor community as a whole, by providing logistical equipment for establishing such information systems and training and the maintenance of such systems.

To better respond to national developments programmes, including poverty eradication strategies and on a mutually agreed basis, donors have agreed to :

(i) Implement the OECD–DAC recommendation to untie aid to LDCs, which will significantly increase the value of aid in an expeditious manner as agreed in the OECD in May 2001;

(ii) Improve aid transparency through internal reviews and OECD–DAC peer reviews. These reviews may examine indicators to capture the quality as well as the quantity of the assistance;

(iii) Work with LDCs, particularly through close consultations at the national level to better measure progress towards achieving international development goals, which could play an important role in strengthening the impact of ODA on the reduction of world poverty;

(iv) Encourage greater participation of recipient countries in discussion on international aid policy in order to strengthen partnerships and enhance the effectiveness of ODA;

(v) Seek to enhance the value of their development assistance by increasing the proportion of goods and services sourced in the recipient LDC or from other LDCs or developing countries to help boost pro-poor economic growth in these countries.

(C) External Debt

The external debt overhang in the majority of LDCs constitutes a serious obstacle to their development efforts and economic growth. Debt service takes up a large part of scarce budgetary resources that could be directed to productive and social areas, and the debt overhang harms the internal and external investment climate. The situation is aggravated further by effects of external financial turbulence, volatility of export earnings, and increases in the prices of essential imports. Since the Second UN Conference on LDCs, the total amount of LDCs' debt has increased.

The serious debt problems of LDCs necessitates a comprehensive solution, including the full, speedy and effective implementation of the enhanced HIPC initiative and other debt relief measures, to address structural causes of indebtedness, and provision of ODA, with a view to ensuring that these countries do not fall back into arrears. The full implementation of these actions is crucial. Actions taken by multilateral and bilateral creditors to provide faster, deeper and broader debt relief for HIPC are useful steps towards solving serious debt problems. The steps taken by the donor community, particulars by members of the Paris Club and other bilateral creditors, to address external debt problems, including a moratorium on debt service payments by LDCs, are welcome. The debtor LDCs will aim at maximizing benefits from debt relief by creating a conducive national framework including fiscal reforms, a budgetary framework, suctorial adjustments, contributing to poverty eradication and faster economic growth, export growth, increased investment, enhanced productive capacities, employment and productivity, savings and international competitiveness. Efforts should be continued through transparent procedures to monitor and review LDCs' debt sustainability on the basis of appropriate and objective criteria.

Action by LDCs and the development partners will be along the following lines :

1. Action by LDCs

(i) Taking measures to enhance a conducive national policy framework that contributes effectively to poverty eradication and promotes faster economic growth, including fiscal reforms, adjustments, faster export growth and increasing investment, productive capacities, employment and productivity, savings and international competitiveness;

(ii) Using resources released by debt relief as well as other sources of development finance in a manner that fully takes into account the interests of the poor and also promotes long-term economic growth and beneficial integration of LDCs into global economy;

(iii) Designing and implementing nationally-owned development policies and strategies including, where appropriate, Poverty Reduction Strategy Papers (PRSPs), with full participation of all stakeholders;

(iv) Initiating joint action with their development partners on the debt situation including a comprehensive assessment of their debt problems and debt sustainability;

(v) Sustaining and intensifying effort to improve debt management capability *inter alia* by regularly consulting with creditors and development partners on the debt problem.

2. Action by Development Partners

(i) Effectively implementing the enhanced HIPC Initiative and providing adequate financial resources expeditiously for the speedy and full implementation of the enhanced HIPC initiative, and providing new and additional resources necessary to fulfill the future financial requirements of the enhanced HIPC Initiative, on the basis of fair and equitable burden-sharing;

(ii) Encouraging Non-Paris Club official to participate in debt relief measures to assist LDCs;

(iii) Making expeditious progress towards full cancellation, in the context of enhanced HIPC, of outstanding official bilateral debt owned by HIPC LDCs;

(iv) Implementing the enhanced programme of debt relief for the heavily indebted poor countries without further delay and agreeing to cancel all official bilateral debts of those countries in return for their making demonstrable commitments to poverty eradication;

(v) Writing off multilateral debt in the context of the enhanced HIPC for LDCs that are HIPCs should be a high priority, and mobilizing sufficient resources for this purpose;

(vi) Considering on a case by case basis debt relief measures for LDCs which are not HIPCs as an integral part of development processes;

(vii) Providing debt relief to post-conflict countries under the enhanced HIPC as soon as possible, within the flexibility provided under HIPC framework;

(viii) Encouraging creditors in a position to do so to consider a moratorium on debt service payments for LDCs in exceptions cases;

(ix) Reviewing and continuing to monitor LDCs' debt sustainability in the appropriate fora on the basis of objective criteria and transparent analysis;

(x) Actively assisting LDCs to build their capacities in the area of debt management;

(xi) Assisting LDCs in their efforts to use resources released by debt relief as well as other sources of development finance in a manner that fully takes into account the interests of the poor and also promotes long-term economic growth and beneficial integration of LDCs into the global economy;

(xii) Supporting LDCs' efforts in designing and implementing nationally-owned development policies and strategies, including, where appropriate, Poverty Reduction Strategy Papers (PRSPs), with full participation of all stakeholders;

(xiii) Assisting LDCs in ensuring that the benefits of debt relief are used within nationally owned development policies and poverty eradication strategies with a view to attaining long-term economic growth and beneficial integration of LDCs into the global economy;

(xiv) Considering the implementation of mechanisms for debt relief, such as debt swaps and other relevant debt management and relief tools, with such debt relief fully reflecting priorities of national poverty eradication strategies;

(xv) Assisting LDCs to enhance their capacity to access facilities for commercial debt relief such as the World Bank's debt reduction facility.

(D) FDI and Other Private External Flows

Long-term foreign private capital flows have a complementary and catalytic role to play in building domestic supply capacity as they lead to tangible and intangible benefits, including export growth, technology and skills transfer, employment generation and poverty eradication.

Policies to attract FDI are essential components of national development strategies. In this context, a stable economic, legal and institutional framework is crucial in order to attract foreign investment and to promote sustainable development through investment. In this regard a conducive international financial environment is also crucial.

Promoting a conducive macro-economic environment, good governance and democracy, as well as strengthening structural aspects of the economy and improved institutional and human capacities, are important also in the context of attracting FDI and other private external flows. Development partners would need to provide a range of support measures, complementing LDCs' efforts to attract FDI.

1. Action by LDCs and the development partners will be along the following lines :

(i) Strengthening the enabling environment for private sector development and foreign investment flows; of particular importance in a supportive regulatory and legal framework for new and existing FDI along with the necessary institutional infrastructure and capacity to implement and maintain it;

(ii) Designing and implementing policies that reduce risks which deter foreign investment, including through the negotiation of bilateral and regional investment treaties and accession to international conventions providing investment guarantees and insurance, as well as dispute settlement;

(iii) Attracting foreign capital, especially FDI, towards the building of supply capacity;

(iv) Encouraging linkages between domestic business and foreign affiliates with a view towards helping to disseminate appropriately tangible and intangible assets, including technology, to domestic enterprises;

(v) Supporting the LDCs in their efforts to integrate the environmental component into national development policies and strategies;

(vi) Assisting LDCs in establishing public-private sector partnerships to address environmental challenges.

E. Alleviating Vulnerability to Natural Shocks

Post-emergency action, using effective and flexible mechanisms, must ease the transition from the emergency phase to the development phase, promote the socio-economic reintegration of the parts of the population affected, remove as far as possible the causes of the crisis and strengthen institutions and ownership by local and national actors of their role in formulating a sustainable development policy. Both LCDs and development partners should encourage the involvement of the private sector, interalia in the areas of disaster mitigation and disaster preparedness.

Actions by LDCs and development partners will be along the following lines :

1. Actions by LCDs

(i) Strengthening disaster mitigation policies and mechanisms, with a particular focus on the poor, especially women and children, and with the involvement of local communities and NGOs in disaster mitigation, early warning systems and preparedness and relief efforts;

(ii) Pursuing or intensifying efforts to strengthen national early warning and forecasting mechanisms, implementing preventive measures and sensitizing relevant parts of the population to the benefits of disaster preparedness and prevention;

(iii) Developing and implementing comprehensive disaster mitigation and preparedness, policies and actions. Such policies should also respond to prolonged disaster with a slow onset such as drought, which often has very severe economic, environmental and social impacts;

(iv) Considering the creation of innovative financial instruments, such as special insurance schemes, to facilitate post-disaster reconstruction with a view to maintaining standards of living and productive capacities in the LDCs.

(a) Action by Development Partners

(i) Giving priority attention to the LDCs in the substantive programme and institutional arrangements for implementing the new International Strategy for Disaster Reduction;

(ii) Providing assistance for disaster mitigation, at the request of affected countries, as well as for improving the capacity of LDCs to identify mitigation scenarios and establishing protective measures and contingency plans;

(iii) Supporting LDCs enhancement of capacity to effectively participate in and benefit from regional and international early warning and disaster mitigation and response networks, including through satellite—driven technologies.

(iv) Sharing operationally useful disaster information, including satellite data, as widely as possible within the international disaster relief community, through appropriate programmes such as the UN website ReliefWeb.

ANNEXURE III-14

Relevant Extracts from Action Programme Regarding Increasing Trade of LDCs

COMMITMENT 5: ENHANCING THE ROLE OF TRADE IN DEVELOPMENT

Trade will increasingly continue to be relied upon by LDCs generate the resources for financing growth and development to complement those from ODA and private capital flows. The share of trade in GDP remains relatively high in most LDCs compared with other developing countries. However, the participation of LDCs in international trade is severely limited by the number of factors, in particular demand and supply-side constraints, as well as unfavourable market access conditions in markets affecting the products of greatest export interest to them, which largely explain their marginal share of 0.4 per cent of world trade in 1998. Coping with increased global market competitiveness also presents an important and great policy challenge to LDCs, and how they respond to it will be decisive in their success in regional and global integration strategies. Concrete action by the LDCs themselves, as well as their development partners, will therefore be required in order to overcome these constraints and transform trade into a powerful engine for growth and poverty eradication, as well as an effective instrument for drawing benefits from globalisation and trade liberalisation. Coherent actions by the United Nations, the Bretton Woods institutions and the World Trade Organisation along with the action of Government remain an essential element of overall policy reform. Integration into the world economy is an insufficient but necessary precondition for long-term sustainability of poverty eradication. Integration of LDCs into the global economy can only be achieved through an integrated approach, including trade and macroeconomic policy, private sector development, finance, infrastructure, education and other supply-side measures. Regional integration compatible with multimedia trade rules, can be an important stepping stone for LDCs to integrate themselves into the world economy and can help make liberalisation work by enhancing the credibility and transparency of policy reforms. Regional integration can contribute to increasing the size of markets and thus make them more attractive to FDI.

(A) Trade Commodities and Regional Trading Arrangement

The actions below relate to external trade and related areas, commodities and regional trading arrangements, and should be read in conjunction with policies and actions under other commitments.

1. Actions by LDCs

(i) Strengthening efforts to integrate policies into national development policies towards poverty eradication.

(ii) Capacity-building in trade policy and related areas such as tariffs, customs, competition, investment and technology, including through the use of the Integrated Framework for Trade-related Technical Assistance for LDCs.

(iii) Improving economic openness and policy predictability, as well as sound macro-economic policy.

(iv) Developing economic and institutional capacities for effective and informed participation in the multilateral trading system and for effective negotiations on trade, finance, technology transfer and related areas.

(v) Removing procedural and institutional bottlenecks that increase transaction costs, including through efforts to improve efficiency, efficacy and transparency by the implementation of trade facilitation measures and improving standards and quality control.

(vi) Taking advantage of market access opportunities through the identification and strengthening of lead subsectors in order to exploit actual and potential supply capacity.

(vii) Promoting trade and the competitiveness of exports in order to facilitate the integration of domestic enterprise into the international economy.

(viii) Intensifying horizontal and vertical diversification, including local processing of primary commodities.

(ix) Promoting sub-regional and regional cooperation, including for export promotion, and improving transport infrastructure to reduce costs and increase trade flows, taking into account the needs of landlocked LDCs and transit neighbours.

(x) Implementing measures to enable women in LDCs

especially women entrepreneurs, to exploit the opportunities created by trade policy reforms and to mitigate and negative effects on them of these reforms.

(xi) Ensuring that food, agricultural trade, and overall trade policies are conducive to fostering food security for all through fair and market oriented agricultural trading system.

2. *Actions by Development Partners*

Developing partners will aim, including through actions within relevant multilateral for a, at :

(i) Assisting LDCs in capacity-building in trade policy and related areas such as tariffs, customers, competition, investment and technology, particularly through the use of the Integrated Framework for Trade-related Technical Assistance for LDC.

(ii) Assisting LDCs in developing human and institutional capacities for effective negotiations and informed participation in multilateral trading system in order that LDCs reap maximum benefits from it;

(iii) Assisting LDCs in removing precedural and institutional bottlenecks that increase transaction costs, including efforts to improve efficiency, efficacy and transparency by the implementation of trade facilitation measures and improving standards and quality control.

(iv) Assisting LDCs in intensifying horizontal and vertical diversification including local processing of primary commodities.

(v) Providing financial, technical and/or other forms of assistance in support of LDCs' efforts to improve their transport infrastructure, particularly the efforts of island and lacklocked LDCs, so as to reduce costs and increase trade flows :

(vi) Supporting inter alia through financial and/or other forms of assistance, LDC's efforts to promote sub regional and regional cooperation, including for export promotion.

(vii) Assisting LDCs in their efforts to implement measures to enable women in LDCs, especially women entrepreneurs, to exploit the opportunities created by trade policy reforms and to mitigate any negative effects on them of these reforms.

Market Access

(viii) Improving preferential market access for LDCs by working towards the objective of duty-fee and quota-free market access for all LDCs' products. This will apply in the markets of developed countries. Improvements in market access for LDCs should be granted on a secure and predictable basis. They should be combined with simplified rules of origin that provide transparency and predictability so as to help ensure that LDCs benefit from the market access granted, and multi-donor programmes, such as the Integrated Framework for Trade-related Technical Assistance (IF), to upgrade LDCs' production and export capacities and capabilities. Consideration should be given to proposals for developing countries to contribute to improve market access for LDCs' exports.

Special and Differential Treatments

(ix) Implementing in full and as a matter of priority the special and differential measures in favour of LDCs as contained in the Final Act of the Urguay Round New Measures for LDCs should also be considered as part of future multilateral trade negotiations.

(x) Continuing to improve the Generalised System of Preferences (GSP) for LDCs, inter alia by reducing administrative and procedural complexities and by making it more predictable.

(xi) In any appropriate negotiations, examining the possibility of strengthening the effectiveness of non-actionable categories of subsidies in order to take into account the needs of LDCs.

(xii) Increasing support to enhance agriculture production and productivity.

(xiii) Strengthening as required, technical assistance for the implementation of multilateral trade agreements and considering making such technical assistance an integral part of commitments to be taken in future trade agreements. Technical cooperation in areas related to the implementation of existing or possible new WTO agreements should complement LDCs' trade policy reforms.

(xiv) Providing technical assistance for the implementation of the WTO agreements on Technical Barriers to trade and on Sanitary and Phytosanitary Measures with a view to responding to the special problems faced by the LDCs.

Accession to WTO

(xv) As some developing countries, including a considerable number of LDCs, are not members of WTO, facilitating the accession process on the basis of terms that take into account their stage of development and the basic principles of special and differential treatment. In the meantime, supporting efforts of LDCs already seeking to accede, which will include.

(i) Ensuring that the accession process is more effective and less onerous and tailored to their specific economic conditions, inter alia by streamlining WTO procedural requirements.

(ii) Providing for automatic eligibility of all acceding LDCs for all provisions on special and different treatment in existing WTO agreements.

(iii) In view of LDCs' special economic situation and their development, financial and trade needs, WTO members should exercise restraint, where appropriate, in seeking concessions in the negotiations on market access for goods and services in keeping with the letter and spirit of the market provisions of the Ministerial Decision on Measures in Favour of the Least Development Countries.

(iv) Seeking from LDCs in the accession stage only commitments that are commensurate with their level of development.

(v) Continuing to provide adequate and predictable assistance to LDCs for their accession process, including technical, financial or other forms of assistance.

(vi) Accelerating the accession process for LDCs that are in the process of accession to WTO.

Standard-setting and Quality Control

(xvi) Continuing to provide support for effective participation by LDCs in international standard-setting organisations in order to address their concerns.

(xvii) Providing assistance to LDCs in developing infrastructure to ensure quality control and conformity with international standards of their products.

(xviii) Adhering to international standards, guidelines and recommendations when applying sanitary and phyto-sanitary (SPS) measures and other technical standards as laid out in the SPS Agreement, and avoiding taking unilateral actions in a manner inconsistent with the Agreement.

(xix) Taking measures, where appropriate, to compensate for trade losses incurred by the LDCs as a result of unilateral SPS trade measures found to be inconsistent with the SPS Agreement, or, in the case of disputes among non-WTO members, measures inconsistent with agreed international standards and guidelines.

Commodities

(xx) LDCs are particularly vulnerable to high fluctuations in resource flows through their exposure to external terms of trade shocks. The recent downward swing in the prices of primary commodities and the upward swing in petroleum prices are only the latest examples of the effect of volatility of commodity prices on the poorest countries. Diversification of the export base would therefore help LDCs to overcome one of the most important weaknesses of their development. Furthermore, economic development in LDCs would benefit from policies aimed at developing the informal sector and the small and medium-size enterprises in LDCs.

(xxi) Supporting capacity building in the areas of research and development, production, processing and marketing of commodities, including addition of non-traditional commodities where market niches offer fresh opportunities.

(xxii) Supporting diversification programmes in LDCs including by strengthening activities covered by the Second Account of the Common Fund for Commodities and adaptive Research and Development (R&D) on production and processing aimed particularly at small holders and small and medium-sized enterprises in these countries.

(xxiii) Continuing to provide technical and financial support to enhance the productive capacities of LDCs through stimulating investment, human resources development and enhancing technological capacities with a view to increasing the commodity exports of LDCs.

(xxiv) Providing assistance, including financial, technical and/ or other forms of assistance, to LDCs in their efforts to create essential infrastructure to facilitate the functioning of liberalised domestic and regional markets.

(xxv) Encouraging private sector initiatives and supporting the establishment of partnerships with foreign companies as inter alia a vehicle for the transfer of production and marketing skills.

(xxvi) Supporting LDCs' efforts in building institutional and technical capacities to gain access to and make use of modern risk management techniques and tools.

(xxvii) Continuing to provide compensatory financing in order to mitigate adverse consequences of commodity price volatility on LDC economics.

(xxviii) Supporting LDCs' efforts to develop and take advantage of niche markets for goods such as horticultural, meat fish and organic products and handicrafts, as well as cultural products.

Regional Trading Arrangements

(xxix) Taking appropriate account in regional integration arrangements of particular constraints that LDCs face as a result of their different level of development and supporting them to enhance their production, supply and trading capacities, as well as their capacity to attract investment; providing support to the process of trade and investment liberalisation and macro-economic and structural policy reform, as well as programmes at the regional level intended to enhance the benefits of integration for LDCs; and providing support to concrete joint subregional trade projects involving LDCs and non-LDCs participating in a subregional trade arrangement and intended to enhance the benefits of integration for LDCs.

(xxx) Making use of the flexibilities provided for in multilateral trade rules relating to regional trade arrangements involving LDCs with the aim of fostering their smooth and beneficial integration into the world economy.

Integrated Framework (IF) and other Trade-related Technical Assistance in Country-specific Strategies

(xxxi) Integrating trade and trade-related technical assistance in country-specific strategies.

(xxxii) Implementing expeditiously and effectively the Integrated Framework for Trade-related Technical Assistance for LDCs, taking account of the pilot scheme.

(xxxiii) Encouraging new and additional contributions to the IF Trust Fund, as well as providing stable and predictable funding for the implementation of Integrated Framework, including where appropriate considering an increase from the regular budgets of the core agencies, as well as through bilateral programmes.

(xxxiv) Continuing to implement existing programmes for coordinated trade related technical assistance such as the Joint Integrated Technical Assistance Programme (JITAP) by providing systematic and sustained assistance to the programme and considering expanding it to cover other African LDCs.

(xxxv) Providing technical and financial assistance to help LDCs create institutional and human capacities in production, processing and increasing domestic value-added, marketing and management know-how in the field of international trade.

(B) Service

Services such as tourism, transport and business services are increasingly important to LDCs, both as a direct source of foreign exchange earning and for the expansion of the production base and diversification of exports, Tradable services are important to all LDCs, in particular to small island LDCs, which have a Limited Capacity for merchandise production. The development of niche markets for goods or services in which

LDCs may have a comparative advantage represents an opportunity for LDCs to diversify their exports.

Actions by LDCs and the development partners will be along the following lines :

1. Actions by LDCs

(i) Encouraging the strengthening and development of domestic and international services, including the new and emerging ones such as those that rely on telecommunications and ICTs, e.g. data processing services.

(ii) Improving the availability and efficiency of infrastructure facilities to support services trade.

(iii) Establishing appropriate institutional and legal framework to promote development of the domestic supply capacity in services and to ensure the creation of a competitive environment.

(iv) Promoting regional trade in services among developing countries through harmonised legislation in selected services sectors for regional liberalisation.

2. Actions by Development Partners

(i) Supporting through financial, technical and/or others forms of assistance individual LDC efforts to develop the infrastructure for tradable services in which they have a comparative advantage.

(ii) Assisting LDCs' efforts to improve export promotion and marketing.

(iii) Supporting LDCs' efforts in modernising facilities and equipment, as well as upgrading skills in information technology, including through transfer of technology to service sectors in accordance with relevant WTO Agreements.

(iv) Providing support for LDCs in their strengthening of local banking systems and other financial services to make them competitive.

(v) Assisting LDCs through financial, technical and/or other forms of assistance to enhance their supply capacity in tradable services, especially in tourism, air transport and other sectors of interest to LDCs.

(vi) Removing restrictions and enhancing market access

opportunities for service exports from LDCs, as provided for in relevant WTO Agreements in areas of export interest to them.

(C) Reducing the Impact of External Economic Shocks

The LDCs are structurally more exposed than most other developing countries to external economic shocks. LDCs also suffer the consequences of major global and regional economic and financial disturbances and increases in the prices of critical imports such as energy products. The typical export dominance of a single commodity or service sector makes their economies particularly vulnerable to adverse physical or economic shocks.

Actions by LDCs and the development partners will be along the following lines :

1. *Actions by LDCs*

(i) Pursuing balanced policies that seek to limit transmission of external shocks into the domestic economy while promoting gradual liberalisation.

(ii) Developing safety nets to protect the poor and vulnerable segments of the population against the consequences of external shocks.

(iii) Intensifying efforts to improve international competitiveness, including through trade facilitation measures and the use of electronic commerce and other facilities based on modern technology.

(iv) Encouraging diversification in economic activities that are less prone to adverse external economic shocks, based on local competitive advantages Diversification efforts should take place within a broader and integrated approach.

(v) Strengthening domestic financial systems through the implementation of an appropriate framework of rules and regulations, including through adequate prudential and supervisory mechanisms.

2. *Actions by Development Partners*

(i) Pursuing policies that aim at minimizing the risks of adverse external economic shocks and promoting a more predictable and stable international economic environment.

(ii) Continuing to provide contingency and short-term

emergency financial assistance, including balance-of-payments support through appropriate institutions, with a view to assisting LDCs to cope with the consequences of serious external shocks.

(iii) Assisting LDCs in their efforts to strengthen their financial systems.

ANNEXURE III-15

Relevant Extracts from Action Programme Regarding Building Human and Institutional Capacities

COMMITMENT 3 : BUILDING HUMAN AND INSTITUTIONAL CAPACITIES

LDCs' greatest assets are their women, men and chidren, whose potentials as both agents and beneficiaries of development must be fully realised. Efforts at development of human capacities in LDCs have been affected by low and school enrolment and low health, nutrition and sanitation status and by the prevalene of the HIV/AIDS pandemic, particularly in Africa, and malaria, tuberculosis and other communicable diseases, as well as by natural and man made disasters. Making steady progress in this area will be a major objective during the decade. An immediate priority is to focus greater effort on fighting HIV/AIDS, malaria and tuberculosis and their social and economic impact. At the same time, longer-term policies and strategies must be pursued in health, education, employment and rural development, with due consideration for cross-sectoral synergies.

The 20/20 initiative is to be implemented on the basis of mutual agreement and commitment by donors and LDCs. It is recognised that this initiative is important in mobilising new and additional resources, both from domestic and external sources, with a view to facilitating universal access to basic social services.

(A) Social Infrastructure and Social Service Delivery

Actions by LDCs and the development partners will be along the following lines :

1. Actions by LDCs. Education, employment and rural development, with due consideration for cross-sectoral synergies.

The 20/20 initiative is to be implemented on the basis of mutual agreement and commitment by donors and LDCs. It is recognised that this initiative is important in mobilising new and additional resources, both from domestic and external sources, with a view to facilitating universal access to basic social services.

A. *Social Infrastructure and Social Service Delivery*

Actions by LDCs and the development partners will be along the following lines :

1. *Actions by LDCs*

(i) Increasing budgetary allocations in favour of social infrastructure and basic social services, including through intersectional reallocation and appropriate cost-recovery measures, with due consideration for the protection of the poor.

(ii) Creating an efficient environment for and enhancing the effectiveness of social sector investment, including through greater reliance on a participatory local community approach in the design, implementation and evaluation of measures relating to the provision of social infrastructures and basic social services, particularly to improve the condition of the poor members of the community, including through building on deeply embedded traditions of voluntary mutual aid and self-help forms of social capital.

(iii) Offering training, including on-the-job training, to social service providers, particularly to teachers and health-care personnel, taking into account gender equality;

(iv) Encouraging private sector involvement to complement public sector provision of social infrastructure and social services within an appropriate regulatory framework, and seeking lessons from the past in order to avoid repeating failure,

(v) Giving adequate priority to issues of housing and sustainable human settlements in rural areas and in urban locations with a concentration of the poor.

(vi) Making efforts towards the establishment and improvement of national health facilities and statistics.

2. *Actions by Development Partners*

(i) Making determined efforts to increase ODA in support of LDCs' efforts towards provision of social infrastructure and social services, in order to reach the UN social targets in this Programme of Action.

(ii) Promoting and encouraging innovative sources of funding and providing technical support through partnerships among LDC and donor Governments, the national and international private sector, and NGOs and foundations.

(iii) Contributing to enhancing the efficiency and effectiveness of the social sector by reducing aid-related transaction costs and facilitating government coordination efforts among relevant stakeholders.

(iv) Assisting in improving the collection and dissemination of relevant information, including in the establishment and improvement of national health facilities and statistics in LDCs.

(v) Assisting LDCs in developing effective safety nets and swift response mechanisms to cope with natural disasters and socio-economic shocks, including those resulting from economic reform programmes and fiscal adjustment.

(B) Population

The following goals, targets and actions will be pursued during the decade in conformity with the Programme of Action and report of the International Conference on Population and Development (ICDP) and the report of the twenty-first Special Session of the General Assembly (ICPD + 5).

Goals and Targets

(i) Making accessible, through the primary health care system, reproductive health to all individuals of appropriate ages as soon as possible and no later than the year 2015.

(ii) Making available the widest achievable range of safe, effective, affordable and acceptable family planning and contraceptive methods.

Actions by LDCs and the Development Partners will be Along the following Lines :

1. Actions by LDCs

(i) Strengthening population policies and strategies consistent with internationally agreed goals and objectives, as well as with the particular circumstances and demographic trends of LDCs, as an integral part of development policies.

(ii) Strengthening basic health care systems and increasing access to and availability of the widest range of quality health care, including reproductive and sexual health care and promoting reproductive rights are refined in the ICPD Programme of Action, in the broader context of health sector reform, with particular emphasis on maternal/child health.

(iii) Addressing effectively, including through appropriate policies, problems and conditions of labour supply and internal migration.

2. *Actions by Development Partners*

(i) Providing enhanced and strengthened support to LDCs in their efforts to build national capacity for formulating and implementing population and development policies and strategies and to access and use appropriate technology and know-how.

(ii) Assisting LDCs to redress the severe inadequacies in demographic data that restrict effective policy regarding population and development;

(iii) Providing support, including technical, financial or other forms of support, to LDCs to improve conditions of labour supply and mitigate problems of migration.

C. Education and Training

Goals and Targets

Policies and measures will be pursued in line with the following goals and targets.

(i) Ensuring that by 2015 all children, particularly girls, children in difficult circumstances and those belonging to ethnic minorities, have access to and complete, free and compulsory primary education of good quality.

(ii) Achieving a 50 per cent improvement in levels of adult literacy by 2015, especially for women, and equitable access to basic and continuing education for all adults.

(iii) Eliminating gender disparities in primary and secondary education by 2005, and achieving gender quality in education by 2015, with a focus on ensuring girls' full and equal access to and achievement in basic education of good quality.

Actions by LDCs and the Development Partners in Pursuing the Above Targets will be Along the following Lines :

1. Actions by LDCs

(i) Assigning high Priority to education, particularly basic education and vocational training, in developing budgets, to improve access to and quality of education.

(ii) Mobilising national and international political will for Education for All and developing or strengthening existing National Actions Plans on Education, as agreed at the Education for All Conference in Dakar, integrated into a wider poverty reduction and development framework, to ensure that all girls and boys and women and men gain the core skills they need to take advantage of economic opportunities.

(iii) Redressing pro-urban bias in educational policies, where it exists, by actions on both the demand and supply sides, improving curricula and teacher training so that they are gender-sensitive, and improving girls' enrollment at primary and secondary levels in both urban and rural areas.

(iv) Developing and strengthening instruction and technical and vocational training on science and technology, particularly information and communications technologies (ICTs), and exploiting the potential contribution of ICTs to learning including through the use of distance learning.

(v) Taking measures to reduce drop-out rates of children, especially girls, particularly to retain in school children who are poor, vulnerable, disadvantaged and socially marginalised.

(vi) Promoting partnership with the private sector in an integrated system that links education, training and employment, including self-employment.

(vii) Enhancing non-formal education in order to promote adult literacy among women and men.

(viii) Developing an incentive system to attract highly qualified nationals working abroad to take advantage of theirs skills and make good use of their experience for facilitation of networking between the institutions in which they were working and LDCs' institution.

(ix) Implementing education programmes and actions, including public awareness programmes, to address the HIV/AIDS pandemic, tuberculosis, malaria, and other communicable diseases;

(x) Promoting a culture of peace, particularly through education, and strengthening efforts towards peaceful resolution of conflicts;

(xi) Stengthening health education programmes, complemented by immunisation programmes, nutrition, safe water and sanitation and the creation of healthier environments, in recognition that healthy well-nourished children are better learners.

2. *Actions by Development Partners*

(i) Providing enhanced support, including strengthened ODA, from both bilateral and multilateral sources, to reach the above targets on education and literacy;

(ii) Helping LDCs develop or strengthen national plans of action for education, with provision of special technical support to countries facing significant challenges, such as complex crises and natural disasters.

(iii) Providing support to institutional capacity-building for the formulation and implementation of human resources and institutional development policies and intensifying efforts to transfer knowledge and improve the capacity for local knowledge creation in LDCs.

(iv) Supporting systematic reform activities in the education sector.

(v) Encouraging and assisting and tertiary education and technical and vocational training;

(vi) Strengthening local stakeholders working in education, largely through local communities and locally based schooling initiatives.

(vii) Supporting LDC Governments in expanding and strengthening education programmes related to HIV/AIDS, malaria, tuberculosis and other communicable diseases, in partnership with NGOs and other national stakeholders.

(viii) Supporting initiatives to overcome barriers to girls' education, and achieving expanded and improved learning from girls.

(ix) Assisting with efforts, including through technical or other forms of support, to introduce innovative education and training methods, including distance learning.

(x) Encouraging and facilitating networking among educational and training institutions in developed countries and those in LDCs, including provision of voluntary services in educational and training fields.

(xi) Providing financial and non-financial resources for research and development activities carried out in LDCs, including facilitating partnerships between researchers in LDCs and researchers in development partner countries granting incentives to international researchers to participate in R & D activities in LDCs in such areas as health and sanitation, nutrition, education, and other social services.

(xii) Supporting LDCs' efforts in developing an incentive system to attract highly qualified nationals working abroad.

(D) Health, Nutrition and Sanitation

Goals and Targets

Policies and measures will be pursued in line with the following goals and targets :

(i) Reducing the infant mortality rate below 35 per 1,000 live births by 2015.

(ii) Reducing the under 5 mortality rate below 45 per 1,000 live births by 2015.

(iii) Reducing the maternal mortality rate by three-quarters of the current rate by 2015.

(iv) Reducing the number of undernourished people who are unable to reach or to afford safe drinking water.

(v) Reducing HIV infection rates in persons 15-24 years of age by 2005 in all countries, and by 25 per cent in the most affect countries.

(vi) Increasing the percentage of women receiving maternal and prenatal care by 60 per cent.

(vii) Having malnutrition among pregnant women and among pre-school children in LDCs by 2015.

(viii) Substantially reducing infection rates from malaria, tuberculosis and other killer diseases in LDCs by the end of the decade; reducing tuberculosis (TB) deaths and prevalence of the disease by 50 per cent by 2010; and reducing the burden of disease associated with malaria by 50 per cent by 2010.

(ix) Promoting child health and survival and reducing disparities between and within developed and developing countries as quickly as possible, with particular attention to eliminating the pattern of excess and preventable motality among girl infants and children;

(x) Improving the health and nutritional status of infants and children;

(xi) Promoting breast feeding as a child survival strategy.

Actions by LDCs and the Development Partners will be along the following Lines

1. Actions by LDCs

(i) Developing health systems in which special attention is given to the poorest sectors of society by promoting community participation, including, when possible, useful and proven traditional structures, in planning and managing basic health services, including health promotion and disease prevention, bearing in mind the gender aspect;

(ii) Increasing public expenditure and encouraging greater private and community investment to achieve international goals and targets in the area of health, nutrition and sanitation consistent with public policy objectives related to equitable access;

(iii) Implementing policies to improve physical and economic access by all the sufficient, nutritionally adequate and safe foods;

(iv) Embarking on prioritised and verifiable programmes for the prevention, treatment and control of communicable disease, particularly HIV/AIDS, malaria, tuberculosis, diarrhoea disease and respiratory disease, including the enhancement of public health infrastructures.

(v) Giving priority to strengthening the provision of social services related to health care, including nutrition, disease prevention immunisation, education, clean water and safe sanitation.

(vi) Embracing Programmes geared toward proving care for

people living with and affected by HIV/AIDS and for children orphaned by AIDS.

(vii) Encouraging domestic research capacity-building and fully exploiting traditional knowledge systems in the areas of health, as well as adopting best practices elsewhere;

(viii) Developing and implementing prophylactic for preventable childhood diseases and conditions;

(ix) Increasing the availability and accessibility of safe drinking water, particularly for rural populations.

2. Actions by Development Partners

(i) Enhancing ODA and other forms of support, including technical support, for health, safe water and sanitation and supporting LDCs in ensuring access to and availability if safe drinking water by the year 2005.

(ii) Assisting the LDCs to develop sustainable capabilities to provide their people with access to sufficient, nutritionally adequate and safe food;

(iii) Assisting LDCs to set up effective health infrastructures and to increase access to necessary medicines and vaccines, including urging the pharmaceutical industry to make drugs related to communicable diseases, particularly HIV/AIDS, malaria and tuberculosis, more widely available and affordable, particularly for the LDCs, while reaffirming the need for strict compliance with safety and quality assurance and other relevant laws and regulations.

(iv) Recognising and protecting traditional knowledge while continuing discussions on the subject in the appropriate for a;

(v) Supporting LDC Governments in expanding and strengthening programmes related to HIV/AIDS, malaria tuberculosis and other communicable diseases, in partnership with NGOs, the private sector and other national stakeholders.

(vi) Supporting research and analysis on the effects of environmental pollution on human health as a factor limiting economic growth and development.

(vii) Supporting LDCs' Governments in strengthening programmes for control of epidemics, including quarantine processes and infrasctructure.

(E) Social Integration

People living in extreme poverty suffer not only from lack of income but also from lack of access to basic social infrastructure. Poverty fosters social exclusion and exposure to shocks, man made or natural; it also severely limits the capacity to withstand such shocks, which can increase the number of people living in poverty, Actions by LDCs and their partners should include promoting greater social integration and strengthening where appropriate, mechanisms for the participation and protection of all people, including disadvantaged and vulnerable groups and persons. Measures should be taken to ensure respect for and protection of the human rights off migrants, migrant workers and their families, to eliminate the increasing acts of racism and xenophobia in many societies and to promote greater harmony and tolerance in all societies.

Actions by LDCs and the development partners will be along the following lines :

1. Actions by LDCs

(i) Supporting civil society, including traditional and community organisations, in efforts to invest in building social capital and social networks, particular for the poor and marginalised.

(ii) Promoting appropriate legislation for greater social integration and social inclusion, paying special attention to minorities and other vulnerable groups.

(iii) Promoting education programmes that emphasize tolerance based on race, religion, sex, age or ethnicity;

(iv) Promoting diversification of income sources and crop and plot utilisation, with the full participation of those involved at the community level.

(v) Establishing and strengthening micro credit institutions in view of their capacity to make available credit, mobilise savings and provide related financial and business services for an increasing number of people living in poverty, particularly.

2. Action by Development Partners

(i) Strengthening support for policies and measures in LDCs that enhance social integration and social nets, including those which encourage voluntary actions, as well as organisations and mechanisms in the governmental and non-government sectors promoting such policies.

(ii) Stengthening the capability and encouraging the cooperation of relvant UN agencies to promote social integration and social safety nets, particularly in complex emergencies and in post-conflict and disaster management strategies;

(iii) Supporting the strengthening of existing and emerging microcredit institutions in LDCs.

(iv) Proving a greater financial response to United Nations consolidated humanitarian appeals in respect of LDCs.

ANNEXURE IV-1
Estimates of Poverty

Year	*All India*	*Rural*	*Urban*
1973-74	54.9	56.4	49.0
1977-78	51.3	53.1	45.2
1983	44.5	45.7	40.8
1987-98	38.9	39.1	38.2
1993-94	36.0	37.3	32.4
1999-2000			
30 day recall	26.01	27.09	23.62
7 day recall	23.33	24.02	21.59

Source: Planning Commission.

ANNEXURE IV-2

Percentage Variation in Persons Below Poverty Line in Total Population (1993-94 Over 1983)

States	*Percentage of person Below poverty line*		*Improvement (+)/ deterioration (–) in the Period 1983, 1993-94*	*Variation in 1993-4 over 1983*
	1983	1993-4	(col 2-col 3)	(col 4 as % of col 2)
Andhra Pradesh	28.91	22.19	6.72	23.24
Assam	40.47	40.86	-0.39	-0.96
Bihar	62.22	54.9	7.26	11.67
Gujarat	32.79	24.21	8.58	26.17
Haryana	21.37	25.05	-3-68	-17.22
Karnataka	38.24	33.16	5.08	13.28
Kerala	40.42	25.43	14.99	37.09
Madhya Pradesh	49.78	42.52	7.26	14.58
Maharashtra	43.44	36.86	6.58	15.15
Orissa	65.29	48.56	16.73	25.62
Punjab	16.18	11.77	4.41	27.26
Rajasthan	34.46	27.41	7.05	20.46
Tamil Nadu	51.66	35.03	16.63	32.19
Uttar Pradesh	47.07	40.85	6.22	13.21
West Bengal	54.85	35.66	19.19	34.99
All India	44.48	35.97	8.51	19.13

Source : Planning Commission Press Note : Estimates of Poverty (March 1997).

ANNEXURE IV-3

State-wise Per cent of the Persons Working as Casual Labourers to all Workers in Rural India

Sl. No.	*State*	*1983*		*1993-94*	
		Male	*Female*	*Male*	*Female*
1.	Andhra Pradesh	34.96	52.16	43.20	54.60
2.	Assam	17.83	25.57	27.70	48.90
3.	Bihar	36.10	51.21	40.30	59.60
4.	Gujarat	33.41	43.10	43.40	53.50
5.	Haryana	16.10	18.54	24.40	32.10
6.	Himachal Pradesh	11.14	1.18	14.70	1.90
7.	Karnataka	36.86	53.49	36.50	48.90
8.	Kerala	43.09	51.10	48.00	50.40
9.	Madya Pradesh	24.71	33.93	32.20	42.50
10.	Maharashtra	34.26	49.60	39.50	52.90
11.	Orissa	33.80	43.54	37.90	51.50
12.	Punjab	21.30	19.83	32.40	39.50
13.	Rajasthan	13.28	12.33	21.20	12.40
14.	Tamil Nadu	40.69	53.57	46.50	55.80
15.	Uttar Pradesh	18.28	21.51	22.40	24.30
16.	West Bengal	39.02	52.17	36.00	46.00
	All India	29.41	41.12	34.60	45.30

Source: NSS reports.

ANNEXURE IV-4

Growth Rates of Employment in Organised Sector (Per cent)

Year	*Public Sector*	*Private Sector*	*Total organised*
1991	1.52	1.24	1.44
1992	0.80	2.21	1.21
1993	0.60	0.06	0.44
1994	0.62	0.01	0.73
1995	0.11	1.63	0.55
1996	(-) 0.19	5.62	1.51
1997	0.67	2.04	1.09
1998	(-) 0.09	1.72	0.46
1999	0.00	0.11	0.04

Source: Planning Commission.

ANNEXURE IV-5

Elasticity of Employment to GDP

Sector	Estimated Elasticities 1977-78 to 1983	1983 to 1993-94[2]	1993-94 to 1990-00	Project Elasticities As used in 9th Plan Projections	Projected for the future
1. Agriculture	0.45	0.50	0.00	0.50	0.10
2. Mining & Quarrying	0.80	0.69	0.00	0.60	0.00
3. Manufacturing	0.67	0.33	0.26	0.25	0.22
4. Electricity	0.73	0.52	0.00	0.50	0.00
5. Construction	1.00	1.00	1.00	0.60	0.60
6. Wholesale & Retail Trade	0.78	0.63	0.55	0.55	0.50
7. Transport Storage & Construction	1.00	0.49	0.69	0.55	0.40
8. Finance, Real Estate Insurance & Business Service	1.00	0.92	0.73	0.53	0.50
9. Community Social and Personal Services	0.83	0.50	0.07	0.50	0.30
All Sectors	0.53	0.41	0.15	0.38	0.23[3]

Source : Report of Task Force on Employment opportunities.

ANNEXURE IV-6

Growth of Employment by Sectors

Industry	Employment workers (Million) 1983	1993-94	1990-00	Annual Growth Rate (Percentage) 1983-94	1994-00
1. Agriculture	207.23	242.46	237.56	1.51	– 0.34
2. Mining & Quarrying	1.76	2.70	2.27	4.16	– 2.85
3. Manufacturing	34.03	42.50	48.01	2.14	2.05
4. Electricity, gas & water supply	0.85	1.35	1.28	4.50	– 0.88
5. Construction	6.78	11.68	17.62	5.32	7.09
6. Trade	19.22	27.78	37.32	3.57	5.04
7. Transport Storage & Commn.	7.39	10.33	14.69	3.24	6.04
8. Finance Service	1.70	3.52	5.05	7.18	6.20
9. Community Social & Personal Service	23.80	32.13	33.20	2.90	0.55
Total Employment	302.76	374.45	397.00	2.04	0.98

ANNEXURE IV-7

Gross Enrolment Ratio in Classes 1-V and VI-VIII for Major States—1998-99

	Primary (I-V)			*Upper Primary (VI-VIII)*		
	Boys	*Girls*	*Total*	*Boys*	*Girls*	*Total*
Andhra Pradesh	99.20	94.50	96.89	50.86	40.93	46.03
Assam	118.78	100.16	109.63	69.41	52.42	61.12
Bihar	93.20	61.51	78.02	42.43	23.13	33.55
Gujarat	122.92	100.70	112.22	72.06	58.00	65.39
Haryana	82.25	84.05	83.09	67.17	61.09	64.37
Karnataka	111.35	104.38	107.90	70.94	61.06	66.08
Kerala	88.69	87.00	87.86	97.15	93.24	95.22
Madhya Pradesh	119.58	96.46	108.35	75.03	48.09	62.25
Maharashtra	114.38	111.01	112.74	89.28	83.29	86.40
Orissa	109.53	79.82	94.91	64.79	37.43	51.31
Punjab	81.33	84.16	82.66	67.29	65.02	66.22
Rajasthan	125.52	75.68	101.82	78.57	33.60	57.56
Tamil Nadu	109.47	107.10	108.31	97.67	87.94	92.91
Uttar Pradesh	75.97	49.31	63.35	48.88	26.41	38.57
West Bengal	100.06	87.01	93.66	56.99	43.60	50.50
All India	100.86	82.85	92.14	65.27	49.08	57.58

Major States include States with population of 10 million and above as per 1991 Census.
Source: Ministry of Human Resource Development.

ANNEXURE IV-8
India: Health Profile by Gender

Life Expectancy at			
Birth (years)	1971	1981	1994
Male	46.4	50.9	59.7
Female	44.7	50.0	60.9
Total	45.6	50.4	60.3
Infant Mortality Rate			
(per 1000 live births)	1978	1988	1997
Male	123	96	70.3
Female	131	93	72.2
Total	127	94	71.2
Child Mortality Rate			
(per 1000 live births under 5 years age)	1970	1985	1997
Male	51.7	36.6	23.2
Female	55.1	40.4	25.3
Maternal Mortality Rate			
(per 100,000 live births)	1980	1993	1997
	468	437	408

Source: Sample Registration system (SRS) estimates, Office of Registrar General and Census Commissioner, New Delhi, Planning commission and Economic Survey, 1999-2000.

ANNEXURE IV-9
Basic Indicators of Human Development

Year	*Life expectancy at birth (Years)*	*Literacy rate (per cent)*	*Birth rate*	*Death rate*	*Infant Mortality rate*
				(per thousand)	
1951	32.1	18.3	39.9	27.4	146
1961	41.3	28.3	41.7	22.8	146
1971	45.6	34.5	36.9	14.9	129
1981	50.4	43.6	33.9	12.5	110
1991	59.4	52.4	29.5	9.8	80
1996	62.4	NA	27.5	9.0	72
1997	NA	62.0*	27.2	8.9	71
1998*	NA	NA	26.4	9.0	72

Source : (1) Office of the Registrar General of India (SRS).
(2) NSSO Surveys.

ANNEXURE IV-10

Population Covered with Drinking Water and Sanitation Facilities

(Percentage coverage as on March 31)

Item/Area	1985	1990	1995	1998	1999 (P)
Drinking Water Supply					
Rural	56.3	73.9	82.8*	92.5*	98.0
Urban	72.9	83.8	84.3#	90.2@	90.2@
Sanitation Facilities					
Rural	0.7	2.4	3.6*	8.1*	9.0*
Urban	28.4	45.9	49.9#	49.3@	49.3@

As on 31.3.1993

* With Government initiative only under CRSP, MNP, JRY and IAY. Latest authentic data I.R.T. coverage through private initiative is not known.

@ As on 31.3.1997

Note: Percentage coverage in respect of rural Water Supply and Sanitation are based on population covered in current year to corresponding 1991 census population. Percentage coverage in respect of Urban Water Supply and Sanitation are based on Population covered in current year to corresponding current population.

Source: Ministries of Rural Development and Urban Development.

ANNEXURE IV-11

Indicators of Human Development for some Asian Countries—1997

Country	*Life Expectancy At birth (Years)*	*Infant Mortality rate (per thousand Births)*	*Adult Literacy rate (per cent)*
India	62.4	71	62
Kerala State (India)	72.0	12	93
Bangladesh	58.1	81	39
China	69.8	38	83
Indonesia	65.1	45	85
Korea, Republic	72.4	6	97
Malaysia	72.0	10	86
Pakistan	64.0	95	41
Philippines	68.3	32	95
Thiland	68.8	31	95

Source : UNDP – Human Development Report , 1998. For India, estimates are from Office of the Registrar General of India (SRS) and NSSO Surveys.

ANNEXURE IV-12

Central Government Expenditure (Plan and Non-Plan) on Social Services

Item	1992-93	1996-97	1997-98	1998-99	1999-2000	2000-01
Social Services	6397	13659	15894	19729	23727	25873
Education, Sports and Youth Affairs	1878	3988	5012	6550	7115	8416
Health and Family Welfare	1722	2751	3174	3915	5110	5880
Water supply, Sanitation, Housing and Urban Development	788	2957	3304	4190	4619	5087
Information and Broadcasting	371	593	898	1074	1230	1368
Welfare of SC/ST and Other Backward Classes	488	833	725	946	1083	1267
Labour, Employment and Labour Welfare	347	587	562	758	868	941
Social Welfare and Nutrition	803	1950	2219	2259	3702	2935

Contd.

Item	1992-93	1996-97	1997-98	1998-99	1999-2000	2000-01
Rural Development	3211	5081	5583	5403	5185	5397
Basic Minimum Services (BMS) Including Slumk Development	—	2466	2873	3684	4048	—
Pradhan Mantri Gramodya Yojana (PMGY)		—	—	—	—	5000
Social Services, Rural Development BMS and PMGY (1 + 2 + 3 + 4)	9608	21206	24350	28816	32960	36270
Total Central Government Expenditure as per cent of GDP at current market prices	15.8	13.9	14.2	14.6	15.5	15.6
Social Services, Rural Dev. BMS and PMGY as a percentage of Total Expenditure	8.12	11.14	11.26	11.24	10.85	10.72

Contd.

Item	1992-93	1996-97	1997-98	1998-99	1999-2000	2000-01
Social Services, Rural Development BMS and PMGY as a percentage of GDP at mkt. Prices$	1.28	1.55	1.59	1.60	1.68	1.66

Note: Figures for the years 1992-93 to 1998-99 are actuals

. Came into operation from 1996-97.

@ Launched in 2000-01 (BE) as a new initiative for basic rural needs.

.. The total Central Govt. expenditure excludes the transfer of State's Uts share of small saving collections.

$ Ratios to GDP are at current market prices (Base: 1993-94) released by CSO. GDP for 2000-01 are based on CSO Advance Estimates.

Source: Budget Papers.

ANNEXURE IV-13

India: Literacy Rate

Year	*Total*	*Female*			*Male*		
		Rural	*Urban*	*Total*	*Rural*	*Urban*	*Total*
1971	29.45	13.17	42.14	18.69	33.76	61.27	39.45
1981	43.67	21.77	56.37	29.85	49.69	76.83	56.5
1991	52.21	30.62	64.05	39.29	57.87	81.09	64.13
1997	62.0	43.0	72.0	50.0	68.0	88.0	73.0

ANNEXURE IV-14
Selected Indicators of Human Development for Major States

	State	Life expectancy at Birth	Literacy rate** 1991			I.M.R.+	Death rate 1998	Birth Rate
		(Years) @	Total	Male	Female			
1.	Andhra Pradesh	61.8	44.09	55.13	32.72	66	8.8	22.3
2.	Assam	55.7	52.89	61.87	43.03	78	10.1	21.7
3.	Bihar	59.3	38.48	52.49	22.89	67	9.4	31.1
4.	Gujarat	61.0	61.29	73.13	48.64	64	7.8	25.3
5.	Haryana	63.4	55.85	69.10	40.47	69	8.1	27.6
6.	Karnataka	62.5	56.04	67.26	44.34	58	7.9	22.0
7.	Kerala	72.9	89.81	93.62	86.17	16	6	18.2
8.	Madhya Pradesh	54.7	44.20	58.42	28.85	97	11.2	30.6
9.	Maharashtra	64.8	64.87	76.56	52.32	49	7.6	22.3
10.	Orissa	56.5	49.09	63.09	34.68	98	11.1	25.7
11.	Punjab	67.2	58.51	65.66	50.41	54	7.7	22.4
12.	Rajasthan	59.1	38.55	54.99	20.44	83	8.8	31.5
13.	Tamil Nadu	63.3	62.66	73.75	51.33	53	8.4	18.9
14.	Uttar Pradesh	56.8	41.60	55.73	25.31	85	10.5	32.4
15.	West Bengal	62.1	57.70	67.81	46.56	53	7.5	21.3
	All India	60.3	52.21	64.13	39.29	72	9.0	26.4

Source : Economic Survey 1999-2000.

ANNEXURE IV-15

Physical Performance Under JGSY during 1999-2000 Progress upto October, 1999

Sl. No.	*State / UTs*	*Total Works*	*Total Mandays Generated (in lakh)*
1.	Andhra Pradesh	41112	34.71
2.	Arunachal Pradesh	162	1.04
3.	Assam	0	54.49
4.	Bihar	62502	187.55
5.	Goa	220	0.88
6.	Gujarat	4340	10.30
7.	Haryana	7381	7.48
8.	Himachal Pradesh	2914	5.86
9.	Jammu & Kashmir	5555	2.63
10.	Karnataka	40540	73.28
11.	Kerala	22512	13.63
12.	Madhya Pradesh	36048	135.86
13.	Maharashtra	54092	98.63
14.	Manipur	0	0.54
15.	Meghalaya	0	2.76
16.	Mizoram	781	1.00
17.	Nagaland	0	2.03
18.	Orissa	20681	63.69
19.	Punjab	14160	4.15
20.	Rajasthan	9185	26.92
21.	Sikkim	207	0.78
22.	Tamil Nadu	41300	62.51
23.	Tripura	2108	9.08
24.	Uttar Pradesh	30555	108.70
25.	West Bengal	9986	38.98
26.	Andaman and Nicobar Islands	27	0.03
27.	D&N Haveli	0	0.01
28.	Daman and Diu	0	0.00
29.	Lakshadweep	0	0.02
30.	Pondicherry	0	0.00
	Total	406368	947.54

Source : Annual Report : 1999-2000, Ministry of Rusal Development, Government of India.

ANNEXURE IV-16

Financial Progress Under Jawahar Gram Samridhi Yojana during 1999-2000 (upto October)

Utilisation *(Rs. in Lakh)*

Sl. No.	*State/UTs*	*Total Funds Available*	*Total*	*Percentage*
1.	Andhra Pradesh	8172.52	2418.36	29.59
2.	Arunachal Pradesh	493.50	89.08	18.05
3.	Assam	7611.90	3006.90	39.50
4.	Bihar	32019.25	14929.52	46.63
5.	Goa	94.57	86.41	91.37
6.	Gujarat	2908.41	1322.04	45.46
7.	Haryana	2043.13	1112.72	54.46
8.	Himachal Pradesh	805.99	452.47	56.14
9.	Jammu & Kashmir	869.93	189.39	21.77
10.	Karnataka	7173.78	3757.96	52.38
11.	Kerala	3741.40	1262.61	33.75
12.	Madhya Pradesh	14159.28	9479.43	66.95
13.	Maharashtra	12238.52	6022.50	49.21
14.	Manipur	188.03	37.51	19.95
15.	Meghalaya	456.88	180.98	39.61
16.	Mizoram	76.07	68.98	90.68
17.	Nagaland	182.86	85.85	46.95
18.	Orissa	9392.88	3325.23	35.40
19.	Punjab	882.81	563.19	63.79
20.	Rajasthan	3469.37	1780.31	51.32
21.	Sikkim	88.54	57.38	64.80
22.	Tamil Nadu	5758.82	5240.01	90.99
23.	Tripura	429.62	564.00	131.28
24.	Uttar Pradesh	25181.86	9287.63	36.88
25.	West Bengal	12308.04	4229.33	34.36
26.	A&N Islands	27.27	1.45	5.31
27.	D&N Haveli	30.98	0.85	2.74
28.	Daman & Diu	2.05	0.00	0.00
29.	Lakshadweep	8.26	4.03	48.79
30.	Pondicherry	45.96	0.00	0.00
	Total	150862.48	69556.17	46.11

Source: Annual Report: 1999, Ministry of Rural Development, Government of India.

ANNEXURE IV-17

Financial Performance of JGSY

(Rs. in Crore)

Year	*OB*	*Total Allocation Centre + State*	*Total Release (Central + State Share*	*Total avail. fund*	*Expen-diture*	*Percent-age Exp.*
1990-2000	552.71	2205.58	2243.16	2795.88	2035.27	72.80
2000-2001*	624.26	2192.96	1079.41	1703.67	711.35	41.75

Source: Annual Report 2000-2001 Government of India, Ministry of Rural Development.

ANNEXURE IV-18

Review of Physical Performance of IGSY

(In Numbers)

Year	*Works Completed*	*Works under Progress*	*Total Works (2 + 3)*	*Works Exclusively for SC/STs*	*Total Mandays Generated (In Lakh)*
1990-2000	698448	262409	960857	256405	2683.08
2000-2001*	244069	329479	573548	90753	885.12

Source: Annual Report 2000-2001 Government of India, Ministry of Rural Development.

ANNEXURE IV-19

Physical Performance Under JGSY during 1999-2000 (Provision)

S.No.	*States/UTs*	*Total Works*	*Total Mandays Generated (in lakh)*
1.	Andhra Pradesh	63525	133.89
2.	Arunachal Pradesh	606	5.92
3.	Assam	18184	132.86
4.	Bihar	113818	424.90
5.	Goa	191	1.26
6.	Gujarat	24981	44.75
7.	Haryana	14686	18.84
8.	Himachal Pradesh	7848	14.43
9.	Jammu & Kashmir	2910	9.74
10.	Karnataka	76089	175.49
11.	Kerala	31348	37.17
12.	Madhya Pradesh	62939	265.27
13.	Maharashtra	107284	341.55
14.	Manipur	1443	1.11
15.	Meghalaya	0	2.76
16.	Mizoram	1050	2.23
17.	Nagaland	2954	6.96
18.	Orissa	64454	211.51
19.	Punjab	16361	6.62
20.	Rajasthan	21486	105.06
21.	Sikkim	797	2.89
22.	Tamil Nadu	42302	170.27
23.	Tripura	3239	14.49
24.	Uttar Pradesh	193500	438.89
25.	West Bengal	88751	113.83
26.	A&N Islands	43	0.21
27.	D&N Haveli		0.01
28.	Daman & Diu		0.00
29.	Lakshadweep	9	0.11
30.	Pondicherry	59	0.03

Source: Annual Report 2000-2001 Government of Indian, Ministry of Rural Development.

ANNEXURE IV-20

Physical Performance Under Employment Assurance Scheme (EAS) During 1998-1999

(Lakh Manday) upto March 1999

Sl. No.	*State/UTs*			*Total*
1.	Andhra Pradesh	......	......	370.67
2.	Arunachal Pradesh	......	......	38.29
3.	Assam	......	......	147.40
4.	Bihar	......	......	400.89
5.	Goa	......	......	2.66
6.	Gujarat	......	......	63.07
7.	Haryana	......	......	18.02
8.	Himachal Pradesh	......	......	35.45
9.	Jammu & Kashmir	......	......	69.37
10.	Karnataka	......	......	292.41
11.	Kerala	......	......	55.75
12.	Madhya Pradesh	......	......	429.43
13.	Maharashtra	......	......	205.62
14.	Manipur	......	......	16.97
15.	Meghalaya	......	......	10.34
16.	Mizoram	......	......	19.56
17.	Nagaland	......	......	51.59
18.	Orissa	......	......	340.14
19.	Punjab	......	......	19.74
20.	Rajasthan	......	......	209.61
21.	Sikkim	......	......	8.20
22.	Tamil Nadu	......	......	457.09
23.	Tripura	......	......	40.86
24.	Uttar Pradesh	......	......	754.31
25.	West Bengal	......	......	105.26
26.	A&N Islands	......	......	0.45
27.	D&N Haveli	......	......	0.13
28.	Daman & Diu	......	......	0.03
29.	Lakshadweep	......	......	1.62
30.	Pondicherry	......	......	0.38
	Total	......	......	4165.31

Source: Annual Report 2000-2001 Government of Indian, Ministry of Rural Development.

ANNEXURE IV-21

Financial and Physical Performance EAS

(Rs. in Crore)

Year	*Central Release*	*State Release*	*Total available funds including OB*	*Total Utilisation*	*Per cent Utilisation*	*Wage days generated (In Lakhs)*
1993-94	439.10	109.66	548.76	183.75	33.48	494.74
1994-95	1128.52	281.73	1775.26 (365.01)	1235.45	69.59	2739.56
1995-96	1705.69	425.94	2671.45 (539.81)	1720.61	64.41	3465.27
1996-97	1939.59	484.19	3383.34 (959.54)	2160.41	63.85	4030.02
1997-98	1968.72	491.75	3425.88 (964.84)	2307.95	67.37	3816.77
1998-99	1988.45	496.88	3357.88 (872.66)	2819.76	83.98	4165.31
1999-2000 (15 Jan. 2000)	1214.78	404.58	2172.35 (552.99)	928.47	42.74	1202.62

Source: Annual Report, 1999-2000, Government of India, Ministry of Rural Development.

ANNEXURE IV-22

Year-wise Plan Allocation of Funds Under EAS

Year	*Central Allocation (Rs. in Crores)*
1993-94	600.00
1994-95	1200.00
1995-96	1700.00
1996-97	1940.00
1997-98	1970.00
1998-99	1990.00
1999-2000	2040.00
2000-2001	1300.00

Source : Annual Report 2000-2001, Government of India, Ministry of Rural Development.

ANNEXURE IV-23

Financial and Physical Performance EAS

(Rs. in Crore)

Year	*Central Release*	*State Release*	*Total available funds including OB*	*Total Utilisation*	*Per cent Utilisation*	*Wage days generated (In Lakh)*
1993-94	439.10	109.66	548.76	183.75	33.48	494.74
1994-95	1128.52	281.73	1775.26 (365.01)	1235.45	69.59	2739.56
1995-96	1705.69	425.94	2671.45 (539.81)	1720.61	64.61	3465.27
1996-97	1939.59	484.19	3383.34 (959.54)	2160.41	63.85	4030.02
1997-98	1968.72	491.75	3425.88 (964.84)	2307.95	67.37	3816.77
1998-99	1988.45	496.68	3357.80 (872.66)	2882.18	85.84	4279.36
1999-2000	1736.42	593.11	2329.53 (581.14)	2182.60	74.99	2786.17
2000-2001	722.00	171.26	1554.37 (661.11)	650.16	41.83	745.24

Source: Annual Report, 2000-2001, Goernment of India, Ministry of Rural Development.

ANNEXURE IV-24

Financial Progress : SGSY

	1999-2000	2000-2001
A. Financial Progress	*(Rs. in Crores)*	*(Dec., 2000)*
1. Total Allocation	1472.33	1332.50
2. Central Allocation	1105.00	1000.00
3. Central Releases	869.55	274.32
4. State Releases	261.47	136.59
5. Total Funds Utilised	959.86	499.38
Percentage of Funds Utilised to Allocation	65.19	37.48
6. Total Credit Target	3205.00	3205.00
7. Total Credit Mobilised	1056.46	558.46
Percentage Credit Mobilised	*32.96*	*17.42*

Source: Annual Report 2000-2001 Government of Indian, Ministry of Rural Development.

ANNEXURE IV-25

Financial Progress : SGSY

	1999-2000	2000-2001
B. Physical Progress	*(Nos.)*	
1. No. of Self-Help Groups (SHGS) Formed	292426	385443*
2. No. of SHGs Taken up Economic Activities	29017	16956
3. Total Swarozgaris Assisted	933868	44190
4. Percentage of SC/STs Assisted	44.32	44.79
5. Percentage of Women Assisted	44.62	43.23
6. Percentage of Disabled Assisted	0.91	0.73
**Since inception (1.4.99)*		

Source: Annual Report 2000-2001 Government of Indian, Ministry of Rural Development.

ANNEXURE IV-26

Utilisation of Available Funds by States During 2000-2001 (SGSY) (As on 12.2.2001)

(Rs. in Lakh)

Sl. No.	*States / UTs*	*Total Funds Available*	*Utilisation of Funds*	*Percentage of Utilisation to Total funds*
1.	Andhra Pradesh	5191.37	2928.67	56.71
2.	Arunachal Pradesh	288.38	52.74	18.29
3.	Assam	2334.42	323.28	13.85
4.	Bihar	14716.76	5827.84	39.60
5.	Chhattisgarh	3665.22	760.97	20.76
6.	Goa	51.11	1.48	2.90
7.	Gujarat	2815.77	1785.88	63.42
8.	Haryana	1698.78	1193.74	70.27
9.	Himachal Pradesh	741.56	506.57	68.31
10.	Jammu & Kashmir	709.64	330.68	46.60
11.	Jharkhand	4623.00	2398.40	51.88
12.	Karnataka	6075.59	2056.60	33.85
13.	Kerala	4466.81	1044.13	71.18
14.	Madhya Pradesh	6952.99	4454.54	64.07
15.	Maharashtra	13760.73	4046.70	29.41
16.	Manipur	0.00	N.R.	# Value!
17.	Meghalaya	324.56	39.87	12.28
18.	Mizoram	79.47	45.53	57.29
19.	Nagaland	134.93	53.86	39.92
20.	Orissa	8694.74	4325.66	49.75
21.	Punjab	795.81	616.24	77.44
22.	Rajasthan	4578.47	2669.44	58.30
23.	Sikkim	139.67	72.64	52.01
24.	Tamil Nadu	4561.97	3657.45	80.17
25.	Tripura	910.74	428.66	47.07
26.	Uttar Pradesh	25517.57	9789.77	38.36
27.	Uttaranchal	1607.71	58.14	3.62
28.	West Bengal	11103.22	448.84	4.04
29.	A. & N. Islands	35.01	6.23	17.80
30.	Daman & Diu	35.90	0.00	0.00
31.	Dadar & Nagar Haveli	35.90	0.00	0.00
32.	Lakshadweep	35.01	6.23	17.80
33.	Pondicherry	53.59	7.12	13.29
	Total	123736.39	49937.90	40.36

Source: Annual Report 2000-2001 Government of Indian, Ministry of Rural Development.

ANNEXURE IV-27

List of Projects Approved Under SGSY 1990-2000 and 2000-2001

1. Dissemination and transfer of appropriate technology government of Gujarat.
2. Gujarat Gram Haat Comprehensive Marketing Intervention and Support for the rural poor in Gujarat.
3. Setting up to Technology and training development centres government of Andhra Pradesh.
4. Setting up of Permanent Marketing Centres Andhra Pradesh.
5. Infrastructure Development (Installation of Hydrams) in the State of Himachal Pradesh.
6. Vadhan (forest Wealth Baster District, Madhya Pradesh).
7. Development of Muga Silk in Assam.
8. Development of Eri Silk in Assam.
9. Employment Generation through Mushroom Cultivation.
10. Strengthening the Marketing Infrastructure and Establishment of Nodal Centre of Rural Technology in Tamil Nadu.
11. Economic Generation through Coir Production by Women SHGs in East Godavari district.
12. Poverty Alleviation through use of Improved Agriculture.
13. Technology (Expansion of Israel Technology of Agriculture) Special Project under SGSY for Chittor District (Andhra Pradesh).
14. Establishment of SARAS Marketing Centres and Technology and Training Centres in Uttar Pradesh.
15. Mushroom Projection, Uttar Pradesh.
16. Green Banana Plantation, Uttar Pradesh.
17. Nehru Yuvak Kendra Sangathan (Project I for Madhya Pradesh and Orissa).
18. Nehru Yuvak Kendra Sangathan (Project II for Assam and Orissa).

Special Project Approved during 2000-2001

19. Setting up of Handlooms in Bhatinda District of Punjab.
20. Projects Gold Mines-Mushroom Cultivation, Floriculture and Sericulture in Bilaspur District of Himachal Pradesh.
21. Special Project for construction of Water Harvesting structures (Anicuts) in Dholpur District of Rajasthan.
22. Employment Generation through Mushroom Cultivation.
23. Khankhedi Lift Irrigation Scheme District Neemuch.
24. Nehru Yuvak Kendra Sangathan (Project I for Madhya Pradesh and Orissa).
25. Nehru Yuvak Kendra Sangathan (Project II for Assam and Orissa).

ANNEXURE IV-28

Financial Progress Under Rural Water Supply Programme (MNP) During 1999-2000

(Rs. in Lakhs)

Sl. No.	*State/UTs*	*Provision*	*Exp. as Percentage of Provision*
1.	Andhra Pradesh	9283.51	95.46
2.	Arunachal Pradesh	4286.00	48.52
3.	Assam	5535.00	73.80
4.	Bihar	4000.00	5.30
5.	Goa	493.30	53.53
6.	Gujarat	21920.00	62.14
7.	Haryana	3990.00	81.91
8.	Himachal Pradesh	5885.87	84.32
9.	Jammu & Kashmir	7221.27	37.80
10.	Karnataka	7548.79	46.44
11.	Kerala	5005.00	54.73
12.	Madhya Pradesh	10981.14	39.30
13.	Maharashtra	21799.00	61.82
14.	Manipur	1510.89	54.53
15.	Meghalaya	1750.00	53.14
16.	Mizoram	698.00	46.73
17.	Nagaland	1524.00	0.00
18.	Orissa	6111.20	31.53
19.	Punjab	3637.50	28.39
20.	Rajasthan	16300.00	36.75
21.	Sikkim	1115.00	65.88
22.	Tamil Nadu	16544.00	77.75
23.	Tripura	1915.49	63.38
24.	Uttar Pradesh	33703.67	38.95
25.	West Bengal	6500.00	40.04
26.	A&N Islands	1040.00	55.24
27.	D&N Haveli	416.00	63.12
28.	Daman & Diu	206.00	12.23
29.	Delhi	384.00	126.39
30.	Lakshadweep	133.00	62.53
31.	Pondicherry	190.00	38.93
	Total	**201627.63**	**53.17**

Source: Annual Report 2000-2001 Government of Indian, Ministry of Rural Development.

ANNEXURE IV-29

Financial Progress Under Rural Water Supply Programme (ARWSP) During 1999-2000

(Rs. in Lakhs)

Sl. No.	*State / UTs*	*Allocation*	*Exp. as Percentage of Allocation*
1.	Andhra Pradesh	9143.26	90.29
2.	Arunachal Pradesh	2476.00	47.29
3.	Assam	4180.00	79.51
4.	Bihar	9380.00	3.58
5.	Goa	352.92	31.79
6.	Gujarat	6028.52	79.08
7.	Haryana	1883.91	101.45
8.	Himachal Pradesh	2275.77	76.24
9.	Jammu & Kashmir	6381.44	8.99
10.	Karnataka	8402.25	51.40
11.	Kerala	4307.88	75.29
12.	Madhya Pradesh	9444.68	47.46
13.	Maharashtra	13614.41	462.41
14.	Manipur	907.00	9.80
15.	Meghalaya	974.00	65.61
16.	Mizoram	696.00	42.94
17.	Nagaland	724.00	50.00
18.	Orissa	4847.93	40.97
19.	Punjab	1720.64	54.50
20.	Rajasthan	12676.22	40.83
21.	Sikkim	460.83	88.74
22.	Tamil Nadu	6534.66	121.28
23.	Tripura	862.00	64.97
24.	Uttar Pradesh	14775.00	59.39
25.	West Bengal	7008.15	38.55
26.	A&N Islands	12.50	0.00
27.	D&N Haveli	12.50	0.00
28.	Daman & Diu	12.50	0.00
29.	Delhi	0.00	0.00
30.	Lakshadweep	12.50	0.00
31.	Pondicherry	5.00	120.00
	Total	130112.47	97.65

Source: Annual Report 2000-2001, Ministry of Rural Development, Government of India.

ANNEXURE V-1

Millennium Declaration Adopted at the UN Millennium Summit 6-8 September 2000, New York

The General Assembly, Adopts the follwing Declaration :

United Nations Millennium Declaration

I. Values and Principles

1. We, Heads of State and Government, have gathered at United Nations Headquarters in New York from 6 to 8 September 2000, at the dawn of a new Millennium, to reaffirm our faith in the Organisation and its Charter as indispensable foundations of a more peaceful, prosperous and just world.
2. We recognise that, in addition to our separate responsibilities to our individual societies, we have a collective responsibility to uphold the principles of human dignity, equality and equity at the global level. As leaders we have a duty, therefore, to all the world's people, especially the most vulnerable and, in particular, the children of the world, to whom the future belongs.
3. We reaffirm our commitment to the purposes and principles of the Charter of the United Nations, which have proved timeless and universal. Indeed, their relevance and capacity to inspire have increased, as nations and peoples have become increasingly interconnected and interdependent.
4. We are determined to establish a just and lasting peace all over the world in accordance with the objectives and principles of the Charter. We rededicate ourselves to support all efforts to uphold the sovereign equality of all States; respect for their territorial integrity and political independence; resolution of disputes by peaceful means and in conformity with the principles of justice and international law; the right to self-determination of peoples which remain under colonial domination and foreign occupation; non-interference in the internal affairs of States; respect for human rights and fundamental freedoms; respect for the equal rights of all without

distinction to race, sex, language or religion; and international cooperation in solving international problems of economic, social, cultural and humanitarian character.

5. We believe that the central challenge we face today is to ensure that globalisation becomes a positive force for all the world's people. For while globalisation offers great opportunities, at present its benefits are very unevenly shared, while its costs are unevenly distributed. We recognize that developing countries and countries with economies in transition face special difficulties in responding to this central challenge. Thus, only through broad and sustained efforts to create a shared future, based upon our common humanity in all its diversity, can globalisation be made fully inclusive and equitable. These efforts must include policies and measures, at the global level, which correspond to the needs of developing countries and economies in transition, and are formulated and implemented with their effective participation.
6. We consider certain fundamental values to be essential to international relations in the twenty-first century. These include :

- ***Freedom.*** Men and women have the right to live their lives and raise their children in dignity, free from hunger and from the fear of violence, oppression or injustice. Democratic and participatory governance based on the will of the people best assures these rights.
- ***Equality.*** No individual and no nation must be denied the opportunity to benefit from development. The equal rights and opportunities of women and men must be assured.
- ***Solidarity.*** Global challenges must be managed in a way that distributes the costs and burden fairly in accordance with basic principles of equity and social justice. Those who suffer, or who benefit least, deserve help from those who benefit most.
- ***Tolerance.*** Human beings must respect each other, in all their diversity of belief, culture and language. Differences within and between societies should be neither feared nor repressed, but cherished as a precious asset of humanity. A Culture of Peace and Dialogue among all civilizations should be actively promoted.

- ***Respect for Nature.*** Prudence must be shown in the management of all living species and natural resources, in accordance with the precepts of sustainable development. Only in this way can the immeasurable riches provided to us by nature be preserved and passed on to our descendents. The current unsustainable patterns of production adn consumption must be changed, in the interest of our future welfare and that of our descendants.
- ***Shared Responsibility.*** Responsibility for managing worldwide economic and social development, as well as threats to international peace and security, must be shared among the nations of the world and should be exercised multilaterally. As the most universal and most representative organisation in the world, the United Nations must play the central role.

7. In order to translate these shared values into actions; we have identified key objectives to which we assign special significance.

II. Peace, Security and Disarmament

8. We will spare no effort to free our peoples from the scourge of war, whether within or between States, which has claimed more than 5 million lives in the past decade. We will also seek to eliminate the dangers posed by weapons of mass destruction.
9. We resolve, therefore :

- To strengthen respect for the rule of law, in international as in national affairs and, in particular, to ensure compliance by Member States with the decisions of the International Court of Justice, in compliance with the Charter of the United Nations, in cases to which they are parties.
- To make the United Nations, more effective in maintaining peace and security, by giving it the resources and tools it needs for conflict prevention, peaceful resolution of disputes, peacekeeping, post-conflict peace building and reconstruction. In this context, we take note of the Report of the Panel on United Nations Peace Operations and request the General Assembly to consider its recommendations expeditiously.

- To strengthen cooperation between the United Nations to the regional organisations, in accordance with the provisions of Chapter VIII of the Charter.
- To ensure the implementation, by States Parties, of Treaties in areas such as arms control and disarmament, and of international humanitarian law and human rights law, and call upon all States to consider signing and ratifying the Rome Statute of the International Criminal Court.
- To take concerted action against international terrorism, and to accede as soon as possible to all the relevant international conventions.
- To redouble our efforts to implement our commitment to counter the world drug problem.
- To intensify our efforts to fight transnational crime in all its dimensions, including trafficking as well as smuggling in human beings and money laundering.
- To minimize the adverse effects of United Nations economic sanctions on innocent populations; to subject such sanctions regimes to regular reviews; and to eliminate the adverse effects of sanctions on third parties.
- To strive for the elimination of weapons of mass destruction, particularly nuclear weapons and to keep all options open for achieving this aim, including the possibility of convening an international conference to identify ways of eliminating nuclear dangers.
- To take concerted action to end illicit traffic in small arms and light weapons, especially by making arms transfers more transparent and supporting regional disarmament measures, taking account of all the recommendations of the forthcoming United Nations Conference on Illicit Trade in Small Arms and Light Weapons.
- To call on all States to consider acceding to the Convention on the Prohibition of the Use, Stockpiling, Production and Transfer of Anti-Personnel Mines and on their destruction, as well as the Amended Mines Protocol to the Convention on Conventional Weapons.

10. We urge Member States to observe the Olympic Truce, individually and collectively, now and in the future, and to support the International Olympic Committee in its efforts

to promote peace and human understanding through sport and the Olympic ideal.

III. Development and Poverty Eradication

11. We will spare no effort to free our fellow men, women and children from the abject and dehumanizing conditions of extreme poverty, to which more than a billion of them are currently subjected. We are committed to making the right to development a reality for everyone, and to freeing the entire human race from want.
12. We resolve, therefore, to create and environment—at the national and global levels alike—which is conductive to development and to the elimination of poverty.
13. Success in meeting these objectives depends, inter alia, on good governance within each country. It also depends on good governance at the international level, and on transparency in the financial, monetary and trading systems. We are committed to an open, equitable, rule-based, predictable and non-discriminatory multilateral trading and financial system.
14. We are concerned about the obstacles developing counties face in mobilizing the resources needed to finance their sustained development. We will, therefore, make every effort to ensure the success of the High-level International and Intergovernmental. Event on Financing for Development, to be held in 2001.
15. We also, undertake to address the special needs of the least developed countries. In this context, we welcome the Third United Nations Conference on the Least Developed Countries in May 2001 and will endeavour to ensure its success. We call the industrialised countries :

- to adopt, preferably by the time of that Conference, a policy of duty and quota-free access for essentially all exports from the least developed countries;
- to implement the enhanced programme of debt relief for the heavily indebted poor countries without further delay and to agree to cancel all official bilateral debts of those countries in return for their making demonstrable commitments to poverty reduction;

- and to grant more generous development assistance, especially to countries that are genuinely making an effort to apply their resources to poverty reduction;

16. We are also determined to deal; comprehensively and effectively with the debt problems of low and middle income developing countries, through various national and international measures designed to make their debt sustainable in the long term.
17. We also resolve to address the special needs of small island developing States, by implementing the Barbados Programme of Action, and the outcome of the twenty-second special session of the General Assembly, rapidly and in full. We urge the international community to ensure that, in the development of a vulnerability index, the special needs of small island developing States are taken into account.
18. We recognize the special needs and problems of the landlocked developing countries, and urge both bilateral and multilateral donors to increase financial and technical assistance to this group of countries to meet their special development needs, and to help them overcome the impediments of geography, by improving their transit transport systems.
19. We resolve further :

   - To halve, by the year 2015, the proportion of the world's people whose income is less than one dollar a day and the proportion of people who suffer from hunger; and also, by the same date, to halve the proportion of people who are unable to reach, or to afford, safe drinking water.
   - To ensure that, by the same date, children everywhere, boys and girls alike, will be able to complete a full course of primary schooling; and that girls and boys will have equal access to all levels of education.
   - By the same date, to have reduced maternal mortality by three quarters, and under 5 child mortality by two-thirds, of their current rates.
   - To have, by then, halted, and begun to reverse, the spread of HIV/AIDS, the scourge of malaria and other major diseases that afflict humanity.

- To provide special assistance to children orphaned by HIV/AIDS.
- By 2020, to have achieved a significant improvement in the lives of at least 100 million slum dwellers as proposed in the "Cities Without Slums" initiative.

20. We also resolve :

- To promote gender equality and the empowerment of women, as effective ways to combat poverty, hunger and disease and to stimulate development that is truly sustainable.
- To develop and implement strategies that give young people everywhere a real chance to find decent and productive work.
- To encourage the pharmaceutical industry to make essential drugs more widely available and affordable by all who need them in developing countries.
- To develop strong partnerships with the private sector, and with civil society organisations, in pursuit of development and poverty eradication.
- To ensure that the benefits of new technologies, especially information and Communications technologies, in conformity with recommmendations contained in ECOSOC 2000 Ministerial Declaration, are available to all.

IV. Protecting our Common Environment

21. We must spare no effort to free all of humanity, and above all our children and grandchildren, from the threat of living on a planet irredeemably spoilt by human activities, and whose resources would no longer be sufficient for their needs.
22. We reaffirm our support for the principles of sustainable development, including those set out in Agenda 21, agreed upon at the United Nations Conference on Environment and Development.
23. We resolve, therefore, to adopt in all our environmental actions a new ethic of conservation and stewardship, and, as first steps we resolve :

- To make every effort to ensure the entry into force of the Kyoto Protocol, preferably by the tenth anniversary of the

United Nations Conference on Environment and Development in 2002, and to embark on the required reduction in emissions of greenhouse gases.

- To intensify our collective efforts for the management, conservation and sustainable development of all types of forests.
- To press for the full implementation of the Convention on Biological Diversity and the Convention to Combat Desertification in Countries Experiencing Serious Drought and/or Desertification, Particularly in Africa.
- To stop the unsustainable exploitation of water resources, by developing water management strategies at the regional, national and local levels, which promote both equitable access and adequate supplies.
- To intensify cooperation to reduce the number and effects of natural and manmade disasters.
- To ensure free access to information on the human genome sequence.

V. Human Rights, Democracy and Good Governance

24. We will spare no effort to promote democracy and strengthen the rule of law, as well as respect for all internationally recognized human rights and fundamental freedoms, including the right to development.
25. We resolve, therefore :
    - To fully respect and uphold the Universal Declaration of Human Rights.
    - To strive for full protection and promotion in all our countries of civil, political, economic, social and cultural rights for all.
    - To strengthen the capacity of all our countries to implement the principles and practices of democracy and respect for human rights, including minority rights.
    - To combat all forms of violence against women and to implement the Convention on the Elimination of All Forms of Discrimination against Women.
    - To take measures to ensure respect for and protection of the human rights of migrants, migrant workers and their families, to eliminate the increasing acts of racism and

xenophobia in many societies, and to promote greater harmony and tolerance in all societies.

- To work collectively for more inclusive political processes, allowing genuine participation by all citizens in all our countries.
- To ensure the freedom of the media to perform their essential role and the right of the public to have access to information.

VI. Protecting the Vulnerable

26. We will spare no effort to ensure that children and all civilian populations who suffer disproportionately the consequences of natural disasters, genocide, armed conflicts and other humanitarian emergencies are given every assistance and protection, so that they can resume normal life as soon as possible.

We resolve therefore :

- To expand and strengthen the protection of civilians in complex emergencies, in conformity with international humanitarian law.
- To Strengthen international cooperation, including burden sharing in, and the coordination of humanitarian assistance to countries hosting refugees' and to help all refugees and displaced persons to return voluntarily to their homes, in safety and dignity, and to be smoothly reintegrated into their societies.
- To encourage the ratification and full implementation of the Convention on the Rights of the Child and its Optional Protocols on the involvement of children in armed conflicts, and on the sale of children, child prostitution and child pornography.

VII. Meeting the Special Needs of Africa

27. We will support the consolidation of democracy in Africa and assist Africans in their struggle for lasting peace, poverty eradication and sustainable development, thereby bringing Africa into the mainstream of the world economy.
28. We resolve, therefore :

- To give full support to the political and institutional structures of emerging democracies in Africa.

- To encourage and sustain regional and subregional mechanisms for preventing conflict and promoting political stability, and to ensure a reliable flow of resources for peacekeeping operations on the continent.
- To take special measures to address the challenges of poverty eradication and sustainable development in Africa, including debt cancellation, improved market access, enhanced Official Development Assistance (ODA), and increased flows of Foreign Direct Investment (FDI) as well as transfers of technology.
- To help Africa build up its capacity to tackle the spread of the HIV/AIDS pandemic and other infectious diseases.

VIII. Strengthening the United Nations

29. We will spare no effort to make the United Nations a more effective instrument for pursuing all of these priorities; the fight for development for all the peoples of the world, the fight against poverty, ignorance and disease; the fight against injustice; the fight against violence, terror and crime; and the fight against the degradation and destruction of our common home.

30. We resolve therefore :

    - To reaffirm the central position of the General Assembly as the chief deliberative, policy-making and representative organ of the United Nations, and to enable it to play that role effectively.
    - To intensify our efforts to achieve a comprehensive reform of the Security Council in all its aspects.
    - To further strengthen the Economic and Social Council, building on its recent achievements, to help it fulfill the role ascribed to it in the Charter.
    - To strengthen the International Court of Justice, in order to ensure justice and the rule of law in international affairs.
    - To encourage regular consultations and coordination among the principle organs of the United Nations in pursuit of their functions.
    - To ensure that the Organisation is provided on a timely and predictable basis with the resources it needs to carry out its mandates.

- To urge the Secretariat to make the best use of those resources, in accordance with clear rules and procedures agreed by the General Assembly, in the interests of all Member States, by adopting the best management practices and technologies available and by concentrating on those tasks that reflect the agreed priorities of Member States.
- To promote adherence to the Convention on the Safety of United Nations and Associated Personnel.
- To ensure greater policy coherence and to improve better cooperation between the United Nations, its agencies, the Bretton Woods Institutions, and the World Trade Organisation, as well as other multilateral bodies, with a view to achieving a fully coordinated approach to the problems of peace and development.
- To further strengthen cooperation between the United Nations and National Parliaments through their world organisation, the Inter-Parliamentary Union, in various fields, including : peace and security, economic and social development, international law and human rights, democracy and gender issues.
- To give greater opportunities to the private sector, non-governmental organisations and civil society in general, to contribute to the realization of the Organisation's goals and programmes.

31. We request the General Assembly to review on a regular basis the progress made in implementing the provisions of this Declaration, and ask the Secretary—General to issue periodic reports, for consideration by the General Assembly and as a basis for further action.
32. We solemnly reaffirm, on this historic occasion, that the United Nations is the indispensable common house of the entire human family, through which we will seek to realize our universal aspirations for peace, cooperation and development. We, therefore, pledge our unstinting support for these common objectives, and our determination to achieve them.

ANNEXURE V-2

Extracts from Action Programme Regarding Policies to Make Globalisation Work for LDCs

COMMITMENT-4 : BUILDING PRODUCTIVE CAPACITIES TO MAKE GLOBALISATION WORK FOR LDCs

The capacity of LDCs to accelerate growth and sustainable development is impeded by various structural and supply-side constraints. Among these constraints are low productivity; insufficient financial resources; inadequate physical and social infrastructure; lack of skilled human resources; degradation of the environment; weak institutional capacities, including trade support services, in both public and private sectors; low technological capacity; lack of an enabling environment to support entrepreneurship and promote public and private partnership; and lack of access of the poor, particularly women, to productive resources and services. Geographical handicaps faced by landlocked and island LDCs aggravate the impact of these impediments. Critical factors to stimulate productive capacity include : stable macro-economic conditions, a conductive legal and regulatory framework, adequate institutional, physical and social infrastructure and a vibrant private sector. An effective dialogue between government and the private sector, as well as policy consistency within trade, investment and enterprise development, is needed to underpin an enabling environment for economic development. It is also important to encourage and promote good corporate practices. Concrete support should be based upon the national programmes of action or poverty eradication strategies of LDCs.

The following goals and targets may be pursued, in accordance with national development policies and strategies.

(i) Increasing road networks or connections in LDCs to the current level of other developing countries and urban road capacities, including sewerage and other related facilities, by 2010.

(ii) Modernizing and expanding ports and airports and their ancillary facilities to enhance their capacities by 2010.

(iii) Modernizing and expanding railway connections and

facilities, increasing their capacities to the level of those in other developing countries by the end of the decade;

(iv) Increasing LDC's communication networks, including telecommunication and postal services, and improving access of the poor to such services in urban and rural areas to reach the current levels in other developing countries.

(v) Increasing computer literacy among students in higher institutions and universities by 50 per cent and in junior and high schools by 25 per cent by 2015.

(vi) Increasing average telephone density to 5 main lines per 100 inhabitants and Internet connections to 10 users per 100 inhabitants by the year 2010.

A paramount objective of the actions by LDCs and their development partners should be to continue to strengthen productive capacities by overcoming structural constraints. Access to finance by way of domestic resource mobilisation, foreign direct investment and increased ODA resources will be critical in this regard. LDCs should be treated with flexibility in the application of relevant multilateral disciplines, without compromising those disciplines, so as to allow them a degree of freedom in providing appropriate incentives with a view to improving productive capacity, diversification, and export capability and raising competitiveness.

In the LDCs, national development programmes can be effective only if they attempt to address the supply capacity weaknesses of this group of countries. The ongoing process of globalisation and interdependence is potentially a powerful and dynamic force that can contribute to growth, poverty eradication and sustainable development for LDCs. However, the LDCs have not been able to take full advantage of these opportunities, owing to supply and demand side constraints facing them. Strong actions are therefore required to help LDCs to integrate beneficially into the world economy, reversing their marginalisation in global trade, finance, investment and technology flows. In this respect, addressing supply capacity weaknesses by building productive capacity will be crucial.

A. Physical Infrastructure

The objective of actions by LDCs and their development partners is to provide a reliable physical infrastructure, which is essential for efficient operation of existing productive assets and enterprises, attracting new investment, and assuring meaningful economic development. The specific Geographical constraints and problems of land-locked and small island LDCs deserve particular attention.

Actions by LDCs and the development partners will be along the following lines :

1. Actions by LDCs

(i) Providing support to the development and strengthening of critical areas of physical infrastructure, including rural infrastructure, transportation, energy, telecommunications, information and communications technologies, and water, including through the encouragement of more private investment.

(ii) Promoting a bilateral, subregional and regional approach to economic infrastructure rehabilitation and development in order to gain economies of scale and attract both FDI and donor funding.

2. Actions by Development Partners

(i) Supporting, inter alia through ODA, LDC efforts to upgrade and develop physical infrastructures, by augmenting public investment in maintaining, upgrading and developing such infrastructure.

(ii) Providing technical support and private sector guarantees to support infrastructure programmes in order to facilitate bilateral, subregional and regional complementarities, including between land-locked LDCs and their transit partners.

(iii) Supporting infrastructure development through inter alia public investment and by facilitating private investment in order to enhance trade, at the national, regional, and international levels :

(iv) Supporting LDCs' efforts to attract private investment and facilitate the transfer of the relevant technology, in accordance with relevant multilateral agreements, for the development of physical infrastructure.

B. Technology

Enterprises in LDCs characterised by employment of low-level technologies, lack of resources to acquire new technologies, and low capability for upgrading old technologies or adapting and utilizing new ones when they are available. Transfer and diffusion of technology by transnational corporations could be promoted by conducive policies, regulatory transparency, market liberalisation and improved absorptive capacity of local enterprises and by addressing the problems of high cost of technology and financial constraints. The very low level of technology in LDCs, including in the areas of new technologies such as ICTs, biotechnology and environmentally sound technologies, will need to be addressed through concerted actions by LDCs and their development partners. LDCs are facing the danger of increased marginalisation as access to global networks, new information technologies and advanced services become driving forces of integration into the world economy. In this context, research and development, including inter alia through the private sector, has a strategic role to play in strengthening know-how and building the necessary special knowledge base in LDCs to prevent a widening digital divide.

Actions by LDCs and the development partners will be along the following lines :

1. Actions by LDCs

(i) Articulating policies and measures to foster an enabling environment to facilitate the acquisition and development of technology and to enhance innovation capacity.

(ii) Attracting FDI that is conducive to transfer to technology, by building up supply capabilities and promoting inter-firm as well as horizontal and vertical linkages in order to foster the diffusion of new technologies within the economy while promoting its integration.

(iii) Promoting appropriate and sustainable technologies by investing in local research and development and capacity-building programmes and by utilizing new and emerging technologies, including the Internet.

2. *Actions by Development Partners*

(i) Through financial, technical and/or other assistance, supporting LDC's efforts to achieve levels of investment in infrastructure for education and training that are consistent with building local technological capabilities, including through innovative private partnerships.

(ii) Assisting LDCs firm to link up with firms in developed countries in ways that would play a catalytic role in LDCs technological development.

(iii) Considering innovative mechanisms with a view to according LDCs special treatment in facilitating acquisition, transfer and development of technology to help LDCs gain access to technology.

(iv) Fostering concerted international partnership to bring the benefits of ICT to LDCs so as to improve connectivity and reduce the "digital divide";

(v) Promoting linkages between research and development institutions in the LDCs and their development partners.

(vi) Complying fully with already existing multilateral commitments in the area of technology granfer, particularly by providing incentives as provided for and agreed in article 66(2) of the TRIPS Agreement.

(vii) Taking concrete measures to facilitate access to or provide technology and equipment inter alia as part of ODA.

C. Enterprises Development

Production in most LDCs, particularly in the private sector, is dominated by smallholder farmers, small enterprises and the informal sector, including industrial and service enterprises which supply most basic goods and services and generate the greater part of employment and incomes. However, the majority of these enterprises have difficulties in expanding into medium and large-size firms, and usually lack sufficient skills and financial and non-financial business development services, access to finance, technology and managerial and entrepreneurial skills.

The private sector can play a crucial role in poverty eradication by contributing to economic growth and creating employment. Specific attention should be given to the needs of micro, small and medium-sized enterprises, including enterprises owned by female entrepreneurs, and to the development of a sustainable financial sector.

Actions by LDCs and the development partners will be along the following lines :

1. Actions by LDCs

(i) Creating an enabling environment for the development of entrepreneurship, including new and innovative forms of financing, as well as targeted business support services to micro, small and medium-sized enterprises in rural and urban areas, including female entrepreneurs;

(ii) Promoting the informal sector through an appropriate legal and institutional framework, including property rights, that facilitates their graduation to the formal sector and improves access to energy, land, water and credit.

(iii) Creating mechanisms for public-private sector dialogue and partnership in order to enhance coherence between trade, investment and enterprise policies and in this regard assist capacity-building of representative business associates.

2. Actions by Development Partners

(i) Complementing the domestic efforts of LDCs by supporting programmes to improve access of informal, small and medium-sized enterprises to financial and business services, inter-alia through public and private venture capital funds and partnerships as well as microcredit mechanisms, and to build the capacity of local sectoral trade support institutions in both the private and public sectors, as a means of transferring and diffusing technology.

(ii) Providing support to strengthen managerial and technical skills and other business support services, including access to information.

(iii) Encouraging public-private dialogue and partnerships with LDCs enterprises to facilitate foreign direct investment flows, including technology and other intangible assets.

(iv) Providing support for capacity-building programmes that provide training, business-development services, networking and partnering, and the institutional framework to foster entrepreneurial capabilities, managerial and technical skills, as well as the growth of internationally competitive small and medium-sized enterprises (SMEs)

D. Energy

The levels of production and consumption of energy in the majority of LDCs are inadequate and unstable. The majority of people, especially in rural areas, have to rely heavily on traditional sources of energy which are injurious to health and the environment. Efficient energy systems are a key element of economic growth, productivity increases, investment in improved technology, lower costs, and a higher level of national welfare. Energy also plays a key role in enhancing competitiveness and in attracting private investment. A strong, efficient, competitive energy sector can support technologies that promote a mix of cost-effective, clean fossil and renewable energy sources for growth and sustainable development. Access to energy transport and communication systems at affordable prices is important to sustainable development and poverty eradication. This will require, over the next few years, large-scale investments and the mobilisation of an important amount of domestic and external resources. While domestic public investments have a positive role to play, in view of scarcities of domestic resources in LDCs, it will also be important to mobilise external capital, including official development assistance and foreign direct investment.

Actions by LDCs and the development partners will be along the following lines :

1. Actions by LDCs

(i) Facilitating the availability of affordable energy, including through the introduction and promotion of innovative financing schemes in rural areas, such as micro-financing and cooperative arrangements for credit and licensing agreements, in order to encourage the involvement of the private sector in providing energy services.

(ii) Enhancing capacities in energy production, trade and distribution.

(iii) Promoting renewable energy development by putting in place an enabling policy environment, with appropriate institutional arrangements.

(iv) Promoting policies that address energy requirements and, in this context, giving as appropriate preference to cost-effective energy sources, including fossil and renewable energy development.

(v) Encouraging regional, subregional and bilateral cooperation in research and development, as well as investment to increase the production and consumption of both renewable and clean fossil fuels and to encourage the interconnection of energy grids.

(vii) Attracting domestic and foreign investments to increase energy infrastructure by creating a predictable and transparent framework of rules and regulations.

2. *Actions by Development Partners*

(i) Supporting the LDCs in their development of energy resources, including renewable energy, natural gas and other clean energy sources, inter-alia through financial assistance and by facilitating private sector investment.

(ii) Facilitating the transfer of technology for the development of clean energy technologies in accordance with relevant international agreements.

(iii) Promoting capacity building in the energy sector, including through national and regional centres of excellence.

(iv) Addressing LDCs' concerns in coping with increase in prices of energy imports inter alia by supporting LDCs efforts to diversity sources of energy, where feasible, and to take measures so that energy policies are supportive of LDC's efforts to eradicate poverty.

(v) Supporting LDCs efforts to diversity sources of energy, where feasible, in order to reduce dependence on any one source.

E. Agriculture and Agro-industries

Agriculture is the pivotal sector in the LDCs, as it underpins food security, foreign exchange earnings, industrial and rural development, and employment generation. LDCs and their partners should pursue further reforms, taking into account the development concerns of LDCs, to improve the productive capacity of agriculture and fisheries, enhance productivity and competitiveness, diversity exports and move up the chain in the processing and export of agricultural products. Increasing the productive capacity of agriculture and fisheries and the income of people working in these sectors in LDCs is therefore a key priority. It requires new investments in regional and national agricultural and fishery research and rural infrastructure, extension of better framing and fishing practices and innovative and sustainable technologies, as well as marketing advice, structured and effective finance and greater tenure security, including access to and control over land by femaled farmers irrespective of their marital status.

Actions by LDCs and the development partners will be along the following lines :

1. Actions by LDCs

(i) Increasing public and private investments in agriculture and programmes for rural economic and social infrastructure, including improving access to rural credit facilities, proving improved investment incentives in accordance with their international commitments, as well as supporting institutions involved in research and development and extension services.

(ii) Strengthening and supporting national, subregional and regional institutions for agricultural and rural development and facilitating their adaptation to changing conditions.

(iii) Increasing access of the poor, particularly women, to support services and productive resources particularly land, water, credit and extension services;

(iv) Encouraging structural adaptations in production, processing and marketing systems so as to respond to evolving consumption patterns and to reduce costs and build on complementarities between production of cash and food crops and livestock, fisheries and forestry.

(v) Taking appropriate measures to implement national programmes of action derived from the United Nations Convention to Combat Desertification, in particular measures to conserve soil fertility and forestry and rehabilitate marginal lands.

(vi) Facilitating access of farmers to appropriate high-yield varieties of seeds for both food staples and cash crops.

(vii) Facilitating access of products to domestic and external markets.

(viii) Promoting agro-based industries as a means to improve agricultural technology, raise rural incomes and foster stronger linkages between agriculture and industry.

(ix) Diversifying production and exports from low value added to high value added products.

(x) Strengthening farmers' capacities so as to improve crop intensity, land cultivation, production, harvesting and storage systems.

(xi) Developing agricultural marketing systems and storage and other related facilities and services.

2. Actions by Development Partners

(i) Providing support for LDCs undertaking to improve agricultural productivity and increase competitiveness, inter-alia through ODA and increased foreign direct investment.

(ii) Facilitating access of LDCs to appropriate agricultural technologies and practices.

(iii) Supporting LDCs' actions for the implementation of the national programmes of action deriving from the United Nations Convention to Combat Desertification, in particular measures to conserve soil, fertility and forestry and rehabilitate marginal lands.

(iv) Supporting the mechanization of agriculture for higher productivity.

(v) Supporting LDCs in developing irrigation infrastructure to reduce heavy dependence on rainfall.

(vi) Supporting development and expansion of social services and physical infrastructure to augment agricultural production.

(vii) Providing support for LDCs R&D policies and actions by, among others, improving access to advanced scientific and technological breakthroughs in the field of agriculture, including biotechnologies.

F. Manufacturing and Mining

Manufacturing is critical to the pursuit of sustained growth in the LDCs because of their potential to enhance technological capacities, advance the diversification of production and exports, add value to exports, and foster intersectoral and inter-industry linkages. For a number of LDCs, mining is an important actual or potential source of foreign exchange earnings. Recent reforms, which lead to modernisation of manufacturing and mining industry, have enhanced prospects of private foreign and domestic investment in mining.

Actions by LDCs and the development partners will be along the follows lines :

1. Actions by LDCs

(i) Enhancing public investment with a view to supporting rehabilitation and sustainable development of the manufacturing sector and fostering domestic and foreign private investment.

(ii) Employing selective, performance-related and time-bound protection of infant industries while seeking to end infant industry protection as soon as possible. Such protection should be used strictly as a transitional provisional provision to address market failures such as public and private monopolies and promote learning and capacity-building for future competitiveness.

(iii) Creating a framework, including by removing barriers discouraging private sector initiatives, that fosters horizontal and vertical ties among manufacturing firms and promotes collective efficiency, stimulates learning, and facilitates their access to infrastructure, training, information and financial intermediation.

(iv) Developing capacity, including through public/private partnerships, to undertake geological mapping, maintain an updated data bank on mineral resources, and provide physical infrastructure in known mineral-rich areas with a view to stimulating private-sector involvement in mining.

(v) Encouraging local processing and value adding, including through diversification, and assisting informal, small-scale artisanal mining to upgrade into organised, formal small-scale mining units.

2. Actions by Development Partners

(i) Supporting LDCs' efforts to increase public and private

investment, and the transfer of environmentally sound technologies on favourable terms, including concessional and preferential terms as mutually agreed and in accordance with relevant international agreements, in the manufacturing and processing sector.

(ii) Providing technical support for geological mapping and compilation of basic data on local mineral potential, product adaptation and market studies for small and medium-scale mines, as well as acquisition of new technologies, skills and modern methods of management by small-scale mining entities, including facilitating LDCs partnerships with private investors.

G. Rural Development and Food Security

Lack of food security is the most typical face of poverty for both urban and rural people in LDCs. Some 70 per cent of the poor and food-increase are rural dwellers, many of whom are small farmers who produce on the brink of survival, or landless people trying to sell their labour. Poverty eradication is critical in improving access to food. Food and nutritional security must be a part of a larger framework of sustainable rural development and of poverty eradication. In many countries, women are responsible for the bulk of food production, but they need the right to own land and to inherit land, inter-alia in order to obtain credit and training, as well as tools, and to increase the productivity of the land and to be able to better feed themselves and their families. All efforts will be made towards advanced implementation of the target of the World Food Summit to reduce by half the number of undernourished people by 2015. The high rate of HIV/AIDS prevalence in rural areas is having devastating effects on agricultural productivity and food security and needs to be addressed.

Actions by LDCs and the development partners will be along the following lines :

1. Action by LDCs

(i) Reviewing and revising, as appropriate, their national plans, programmes and strategies with a view to achieving food security and rural development.

(ii) Strengthening local institutions and enacting policies and legislatin that provide for more equitable and secure access to ownership and control of natural resources, particuiarly land, water, fisheries and forests, by both women and men.

(iii) Strengthening agriculture and rural development support institutions and facilitating their adaptation to changing conditions, in consultation with users and giving due importance to gender-based and other inequalities in access to services.

(iv) Promoting rural industries as a means to improve agricultural technology and raise rural incomes.

(v) Supporting and encouraging grassroots development activities, rural cooperatives and peasants' initiatives.

(vi) Providing facilities for rual credit.

(vii) Continuing the process of liberalizing trade, expanding the sources of food supply and encouraging efficiencies in agricultural production which will expand economic growth and food security.

(viii) Improving transport infrastructure and free flow of information with a view to more effective movement of food from surplus to deficit regions.

(ix) Development integrated nutrition projects from vulnerable sections of LDCs' population.

(x) Undertaking legislative and administrative reforms to give women full and equal access to economic resources, including the right to inheritance and ownership of land and other property, credit, natural resources and appropriate technology.

2. *Actions by Development Partners*

(i) Assisting countries in reviewing and formulating national plans for achieving food security and rural development.

(ii) Providing technical and other forms of assistance of LDCs to attain food security and implement rural development programmes.

(iii) Providing support to programmes and initiatives in LDCs, inter-alia through ODA to improve rural credit facilities and enhance investment in rural economic and social infrastructure.

(iv) Facilitating food security through bilateral, regional and multilateral approaches, including purchase in regional markets in LDCs.

(v) Fully and effectively implementing the decision on measures concerning the possible negative effects if the reform programme on least-development and net-food-importing developing countries adopted in Marrakech in 1994 and endorsed by the World Food Summit in 1996.

(vi) Considering helping LDCs to cope with rising food requirement, including through market-based mechanisms providing insurance for small-scale farmers against sudden terms-of-trade losses on agricultural export markets.

(vii) Assisting LDCs' efforts to boost food production productivity to the benefit of the poor.

(viii) Providing adequate food aid to LDCs facing severe food shortages, including food emergencies, and extending assistance to early warning systems, while seeking to avoid disruption of domestic food production.

H. Sustainable Tourism

International tourism is one of the few economic sectors through which LDCs have managed to increase their participation in the global economy. It can be an engine of employment creation, poverty eradication, ensuring gender equality, and protection of the natural and cultural heritage. These facts principally result from the existence, in most LDCs, of significant comparative advantages that are conducive to viable tourism specialization. Yet, tourism is not among priority sectors for socio-economic development in many LDCs.

Actions by LDCs and the development partners will be along the following lines :

1. Actions by LDCs

(i) Promoting a climate conducive to tourism

(ii) Recognizing the potential of the tourism sector in national development strategies, and ensuring effective participation of domestic tourism authorities in the national decision-making process.

(iii) Determining the most desirable tourism product specialisation in order to guide potential investors in their decisions.

(iv) Promoting domestic and foreign investment in the tourism industry and related sectors with full respect for natural and cultural heritage.

(v) Taking measures to facilitate local tourism operators access to and partipation in global information and distribution systems.

(vi) Formulating strategies to achieve the most beneficial linkages between tourism and land, sea and, particularly, air transport.

2. *Action by Development Partners*

(i) Supporting LDCs' efforts to encourage investment in the tourism industry and enterprise development in the wider tourism economy, in particular through increased access to finance an dthe development of local human resources.

(ii) Assisting LDCs in their efforts to enhance their economic efficiency, competitiveness and the sustainability of tourism operations, in particular by assisting their efforts to access and participate in global distribution systems and use appropriate technology.

(iii) Assisting LDCs in their efforts to promote synergy between transport and tourism, with particular reference to air transport.

Bibliography

CHAPTER I

John Kenneth, Galbraith – 1958 The Affluent Society, Boston : Houghton Miffin Co., Mentor Boon Edition.

Hollis Chenery (Ed.) – 1974 Structural Change and Development Policy : Article entitled 'Growth and Poverty in Developing Countries' by M.S. Ahluwalia and N.G. Carter.

M.G. Quibria (Ed) – 1995 Critical issues in Asian Development : Article entitled 'Income Distribution in Developing Economies by Gary S. Field – Published for the Asian Development Bank – Oxford University Press – New York.

Jean Dre'z and Amartya Sen – 1995 Economic Development and Social Opportunity : Oxford University Press – Delhi.

Foreign Affairs – May/June –1996 Article entitled Globalising Free Trade by C.F. Bergsten.

Foreign Affairs – May/June – 1996 Article entitled, Workers and the World Economy by Ethan B. Kapstein.

Foreign Affairs – July/August – 1997
Article entitled 'The End of the Business Cycle' by Steven Weber.

P.T. Bauer and B.S. Amey – 1957. The Economics of Underdeveloped Countries.
Cambridge University Press, Cambridge.

S. Kuznets – 1966
Modern Economic Growth, New Heaven, Yale University Press.

G.M. Meier – 1976
Leading issues in Economic Development - Oxford University Press.

W.A. Lewis – 1955
'The State of Development Theory' American Economic Review Vol. 74.

D.P. O'Brien – 1981
The Classical Economists – Oxford University Press, Oxford.

J. Schumpeter 1934
The Theory of Economic Growth – Harvard University Press – Cambridge.

A.K. Sen – 1973
On Economic Inequality, Clarendon Press, Oxford.

Economic and Political weekly, Dec. 12, 1998. Article entitled; Amartya Sen and the popular imagination by Prof. Kaushik Basu.

Economic and Political Weekly, Dec. 5, 1998. Article entitled Human Science of Development by Amiya Kumar Bagchi

Annual World Bank Conference on Development Economics – 1996. Keynote Address 'The Role of Government in Economic Development by Joseph E. Stiglitz.

International Labour Review 1996 ; Vol. 135, Growth and Income Distribution in Malaysia, by Robert E.B. Locas and Donald W. Veray.

Economic and Political Weekly dated June 6, 1998 – Article entitled 'East Asian Economies. The crisis of 1999 By V.V. Bhajoji Rao.

Economic and Political Weekly Dec. 5, 1998. Article entitled – 'Economic Development and Political Democracy by Deepak Nayyar.

Annual World bank Conference on Development Economics – 1998, knowledge for Development : Economic Science, Economic Policy and Economic Advice. Article by Joseph E. Stiglitz.

Economic and Political Weekly, March 11-17-1990 – Article entitled Growth, Inequality and Poverty in India by Raghvendra Jha

World Bank
Regional Perspective on World Development Report – 1995 : Jobs, Poverty and Working conditions in South Asia – The World Bank, Washington – 1995.

The World Bank
Article by Gustav Ranis, entitled, Another look at the East Asian Miracle' in the World Bank Economic Review Vol. 9, V 3, 509-534.

The World Bank
World Bank Technical Paper N 328 – Social Development and Absolute Poverty in Asia.

A.P. Thirlwall – 1993
Growth and Development – Macmillan.

Gunnar Myrdal – 1970 – The challenge of World Poverty – Allen Lane, The Penguin Press,

World Bank
Poverty Lines in Theory and Practice-1998 Working Papers

Istvan P. Szekely and Richard Sabot – 1997
Development Strategy and Management of the Market Economy – Vol. II.
Clarendon Press – Oxford.

Subrata Ghatak – 1995
Introduction to Development Economics. Routledge, London and New York.

Deepak Lal and H. myint – 1996
The Political Economy of Poverty, Equity and Growth.
Clarenden Press – Oxford.

R. Lekachman – 1976
Economists at Bay. Mcgraw Hill Company, New York.

Michael Lipton – 1997
Why Poor People Stay Poor : Urban Bias in World Development.
Temple Smith – London.

Gustav Ranis, Sheng Chang HU, (Ed) Yun-Peng Chu – 1999

The Political Economy of Comparative Development into 21st Century : Advard Eiger Ltd. United Kingdom.

Brian Atkinson, Peter Baker and Bob Milward – 1996
Economic Policy
Macmillan, London

James Manor – 1993
States or Markets. Clarendon Press.

Tanji and Chu (Ed) – 1999
Income Distribution and High Quality Growth. MIT

P.R. Brahmanda – 1999
Amartya Sen and Welfare Economics. Sudha Publications, Bangalore

Philip Aghion and Jeffrey G. Williamson – 1998
Growth, Inequality and Globalisation; Theory History and Policy

John Cameroun (Ed) Hans Ram Larak Ken Cole – 1995
Poverty and Power
Oxford University Press, Delhi.

Michael Beaud and Gilles Dostaler
Economic Thought since Keynes
Routledge, London and New York.

Paul Streetan – 1981
First Thing First : Meeting Basic Human Needs in The Developing Countries : Oxford University Press, New York.

Kurt Dopfer (Ed) – 1976
Economics in The Future. Macmillan Press Ltd., London.

Bon Ho AND Dwight H. Perkins – 1995
Social Capability and Long Term Economic Growth
Macmillan Press Ltd., London

Stephen Cr Munday – 1996
Current Developments in Economics, Macmillan Press Ltd. London.

Malcom Gillis Dwilight H. Perkins, Donald R. Snodgrass – 1996
Economics of Development. N.W. Norton Company, New York, London.

Jan Knippers Black – 1999
Development in Theory and Practice. Westview Press

Curt Martin (Ed) – 1991
Strategies of Economic Development.
Macmillan Academic and Professional Ltd., London.

Donald J. Savoie, Irving Brecher (Ed) – 1992
Equity and Efficiency in Economic Development
Intermediate Technology Publications.

Mitchell A. Solgson, John T. Passol Smith (Ed) – 1993
Development and Under Development
Lynne Reinner Publisher Boulder – Clarodo. USA.

Jujiro Hayami – 1997
Development Economics. Oxford University Press.

Jean Dre'ze, Amartya Sen (Ed) – 1990
Political Economy of Hunger. Clarendon Press – Oxford.

Jean Dre'ze, Amartya Sen – (Ed) – 1989
Hunger and Public Action
Clarendon Press, Oxford.

Amartya Sen (Ed) – 1981
Poverty and Femines. Oxford University Press, Delhi.

Amartya Sen (Ed) – 1999
On Economic Inequality. Oxford University Press, Delhi.

Amartya Sen (Ed) - 1992
Inequality Reexamined. Oxford University Press, Delhi.

John Maynard Keyness – 1935
The General Theory of Employment, Interest and Money
Harocourt, Brace and World Inc., New York, Chicago Burlingame

Roy Culpepper, Albert Berry, Frances Stewart – 1997
Global Development Fifth Years After Bretton Woods
Macmillan Press Ltd.

Normal Gemmell- 1987
Surveys in Development Economics, Basil Blackwell

John De La Mothe and Gilles Paquet
Evolutionary Economics and the New International Political Economy Pinter

Stephen J. Savoie, and Irving Breacher – 1992
Equity and Efficiency in Economic Development – Essays in Honour of Benjamin Higgins.

Intermediate Technology Publications 1992.

Timothy Besley – 1997
Article entitled 'Political Economy of Alleviating Poverty. Theory and Institution in Annual World Bank Conference on Developmental Economics.
The World Bank.

Per Ronnas, Orjan Sjoherg, Naud Hemlin
Institutional Adjustment for Economic Growth
Ashgate Publishing Ltd. Gower House, Hampstre, England.

Edmond Maleinvand and Others – 1997
Development Strategy Management of Market – Economy
Clarenden Press, Oxford.

Malcolm Rutherford – 1994
Institution in Economics. Cambridge University Press.

Theodore W. Schultz – 1993
The Economics of Being Poor.
'Blackwell Publishers, Cambridge Massachusette, USA.

Mats Lunda Ed., Benno J. Ndulu – 1996 (Ed)
New Direction in Development Economics Routeledge. London.

Daniel Archewkhgi, Jeremy Howelles Jonathan Michie (Ed) – 1990
Innovation Policy in a Global Economy
Cambridge University Press

CHAPTER II

Growth with Equity, Policy Lessons from the Experience of Selected Asian Countries.
United Nations.

Guillerru Perry, Danzy M. Leipziger, (Ed) – 1999
Chile; Recent Policy Lessons and Emerging Challenges.
The World Bank, Washington.

Santhosh Mehrotra, Richard Jolly (Ed) – 1997
Development with a Human Face ; Experience in Social Achievement and Economic Growth.
Clarendan Press, Oxford – 1997.

Bonho Koo, Dh. Parkins (Ed) – 1990
Social Capability and Long Term Economic Growth
Macmillan Press Ltd., London.

Ulrich Himenj (Ed) – 1996
Growth and Competition in the New Global Economy
Development Center of the OECD.

Mats Lundale, Benno J. Ndulu (Ed) –1996
New Directions in Development Economics.
Landa Routeledge, London.

Wang Shaoguang; H.U. Angang
The Political Economy of uneven Development: The case of China.

UNDP – 2000

UNDP Poverty Report . UNDP

UNDP – 2000
Overcoming Human Poverty. UNDP

The World Bank
Prospects for Development. The World Bank.

Garry Hellenier (Ed) – 1998
Poverty Reduction and World Economy. Macmillan Press, London

OECD – 1999
Waging the Global War on Poverty. OECD

Anish Choudhary and Inytal Islam (Ed) – 1997
Asia Pacific Economic Survey. Routledge

F.G. Adams, and William E. James – (Ed)
Public Policies in East Asian Development
West Port, London

John Cameroun - 1995
Poverty and Power. Oxford University Press, London

UNDP-1997, 1998, 1999 and 2000 Human Development Report (1997-2000), Oxford University Press.

The World Bank
World Development Report 1990, 1991, 1992, 1993, 1994, 1995, 1996, 1997, 1998, 1999, 2000
Oxford University Press.

UNCTAD– 1997 TO 2000
Trade Development Report 1997, 1998, 1999, 2000
Unctad

Vinod Ahuja, Benu Bidani, Francisco, Ferrari and Michael Walton – 1997
Everyone's Miracle? Revisiting Poverty And Inequality in East Asia.
The World Bank.

United Nations
World Economic and Social Survey 1999 to 2000
United Nations.

Vito Tanzi, Ke-Yong Chu, Sanjeev Gupta – 1999
Economic Policy and Equity.
IMF

Roy Chulpepper, Albert Berry, Frances Stewart – 1997
Global Development Fifty years after Bretten Woods
Macmillan Press Ltd., London

Yilmaz Akyuz (Ed) – 1998
East Asian Development: New Perspectives

Frank Cass Newbury House, 900 Eastern Avenue, London IG2, 7HH, UK

Tansi and Chu – 1998
Income Distribution and High Quality Growth
MIT

The World Bank
Poverty Reduction in South Asia – Promoting Participation – Summary of an Informal Workshop Co-sponsored by the World Bank and the South Asian Association for Regional Cooperation SAARC) October 12-15-1993
The World Bank.

The World Bank
The World Bank Technical Paper Number 328 – Social Development and Absolute Poverty in Asia.
The World Bank

The World Bank – 1995
Regional Perspectives on World Development Report 1995 – Jobs, Poverty and Working Conditions in South Asia.
The World Bank

ILO-1996
International Labour Review 1996/5 Vol. 135
ILO, Geneva

The World Bank – 1995
The World Bank Economic Review Vol. 9 No. 3
The World Bank

UNDP – 1998
Combating Poverty : The Korean Experience
UNDP Seoul

M. Kagami, John Hunpheri, Michaell Piore
Learning, Liberalization and Economic Adjustment.

ADB 1999
Economic Openness : Growth and Recovery in Asia
Oxford University Press.

The World Bank 1998-1999

Global Economic Prospects and Developing Countries : 1998 – 1999.
The World Bank

The World Bank – 1998
Annual World Bank Conference on Development Economics
The World Bank

ILO – 1996
International Labour Review 1996/5 Vol. 135
ILO Geneva

The World Bank – 1995
The World Bank Economic Review Vol. 9 No. 3
The World Bank.

Hugh Bredenkamp and Susan Schaldler (Ed)
Economic Adjustment and Reform in Low – Income Countries.
International Monetary Fund.

Michael Bamberger Abdullahi M. Yahie. George Matovo
The Design and Management of Poverty Reduction Programs and Projects in Anglophone Africa. Economic Development Institute of The World Bank.

Asian Production Organisation, Tokyo – 1999
Rural Poverty Alleviation in Asia and The Pacific
Asian Productivity Organisation, Tokyo

African Development Bank – 1998
African Development Report – Africa in the world economy : Human Capital development in Africa economic and social statistics on Africa.

The African Development Bank : Oxford University Press.

George Macesich – 1997
World Economy at the Crossroads, Praeger, Westport, Connecicut, London.

The Asian Development Bank – 1999. 2000
Asian Development Outlook 1999 and 2000.
The Asian Development Bank (Oxford University Press)

Kurt Martin (Ed) – 1991

Strategies of Economic Development
Macmillan Academic and Professional Ltd.

I.G. Patel – 1992
Policies for African Development, IMF

Renee Frendergast and Frances Steward – 1994
Market Forces and World Development
The Macmillan Press Ltd.

African Development Bank – 1999
African Development Report.
The African Development Bank : Oxford University Press.

Bhagirath Lal Das – 1999
The World Trade Organisation : A guide to the Framework for International Trade.
Zed Books Ltd., London.

Akhtar Hussain and Anis Chowdhury – 1998
Open Economy – Macro Economics for Developing Countries.
Edward Elgar Publishing Ltd.

Gerry Helleiner, Shahen Abrahanian, Edmar Bacha, Roger Lawrence, Pedre Malar – 1995
Poverty, prosperity and the World Economy. Macmillan Press, London.

The World Bank –1993
The East Asian Miracle.
The World Bank

Can Africa Claim – 1999
The 21st Century ? 1999 Report by Africa Development Bank, African Economic Research Consortium, United Nations, Economics for Africa and World Bank.

Poverty and Food Security in Asia, Lessons and Challenges – 1998
FAO of the U.N. Regional office for Asia and the Pacific.

Economic and Social Survey of Asia and the Pacific – United Nation – 1999

Tansi Chu

Income Distribution and High Quality Growth MIT

F Gernard Adams, William E. James (Ed)
Public Policies in East Asian Development—Prager Westport, connect cut, London.

CHAPTER III

UNDP – 2000
UNDP Poverty Report. UNDP

OECD – 1999
Waging the Global War on Poverty. OECD

John Cameroun
Poverty and Power. Oxford University Press, London

UNCTAD –1997 to 2000
Trade Development Report 1997, 1998, 1999 to 2000

The World Bank
Global Economic Prospects and Developing Countries : 1998 and 1999
The World Bank

Hugh Breadenkamp and Susan Schaldler (Ed)
Economic Adjustment and Reform in Low-Income Countries.
International Monetary Fund.

Michael Bamberger Abdullahi M. Yahie. George Matovu
The Design and Management of Poverty Reduction Programs and Projects in Anglophone Africa. Economic Development Institute of The World Bank.

African Development Bank – 1998
African Development Report – Africa in the World Economy : Human Capital Development in Africa Economic and Social Statistics on Africa.
The African Development Bank : Oxford University Press.

I.G. Patel – 1992
Policies for African Development : from the 1980s to the 1990s
International Monetary Fund.

African Development Bank – 1999
African Development Report.
The African Development Bank : Oxford University Press.

Gerry Helleiner, Shahen Abrahanian, Edmar Bacha, Roger Lawrence, Pedre Malar – 1995 Poverty, Prosperity and the World Economy. Macmillan Press, London

Can Africa Claim
The 21st Century ? 1999 Report by Africa Development Bank, African Economic Research Consortium, United Nations, Economics for Africa and World Bank.

Deepa Narayan – 2000
Voices of the Poor : Can Anyone hear?, Oxford University Press.

The World Bank – 1998 to 2000
Global Economic Prospects and Developing Countries, World Bank

UNCTAD – 1998 to 2000
Trade and Development Report, UNCTAD

Richard E. Mashomba – 2000
Africa in the Global Economy, Lynne Rienner Publishers : Boulder, London.

UNDP – 1998
Overcoming Human Poverty – UNDP Poverty Report 1998, UNDP

UNCTAD – 1996
Globalisation and Liberalisation – Effects of International Economic Relations on Poverty, UNCTAD

UNCTAD – 2000
10th Session of UNCTAD (19th February 2000), UNCTAD

UNDP – 2000
Overcoming Human Poverty, UNDP

United Nations – 2000
Report of the Secretary General – 54th Session – Agenda Item 49 B – The Millennium Assembly of the United Nations, United Nations.

UNCTAD – 1999
Report of the Secretary General UNCTAD to UNCTAD X-Tenth Session Bangkok, Thailand 12-19 February 2000, UNCTAD

John-Ren Chen (Ed)
Economic Effects of Globalisation, Ashgate Publishing Limited, House, Croft Road, Aldershot, Hampshire GU11 3HR England

Michael Lipton – 1997
Why Poor People Stay Poor – Urban Bias in World Development, Temple Smith, London

John Cameroun with Hans Ranbark and Ken Cole – 1995
Poverty and Power, Oxford University Press – Delhi/Bombay, Calcutta, Madras

UNCTAD - Geneva
The Least Development Countries Report 1995, 1996, 1997, 1998, 1999 to 2000
United Nations

The World Bank – 2001
African Poverty at the Millennium
Howard White and Tony Kellick
In collaboration with
Steve Kayizzi-Mugerwa and Marie-Angelique Savane

CHAPTER IV

Vijay Joshi and IMD Little – 1998
India; macroeconomics and Political Economy (1964 – 1991)
Oxford University Press, Delhi.

International Monetary Fund
Economic Adjustment and Reform in Low Income Countries. IMF

The World Bank – 1997
India, Sustaining Rapid Economic Growth – Country Study.
The World Bank, Washington DC.

National Institute of Rural Development – 1999
India : Rural Development Report.
National Institute of Rural Development, Hyderabad.

National Council of Applied Economic Research – 1999
India : Human Development Report. Oxford University Press.

Ministry of Finance, Government of India 1995 – 2000
Economic Survey (1995-2000).
Ministry of Finance, Government of India.

Research and Information System for Non-Aligned and Developing Countries (RIS) –1999
SAARC Survey of Development and Cooperation
Research and Information System for non-aligned and developing countries (RIS) New Delhi.

Deepak Lal – 1998
India in the World Economy : Unfinished Business.
Oxford University Press, Delhi.

The World Bank
India : Achievement and Challenges in Reducing Poverty.
World Bank Study

The World Bank – 2000
India : Policies to Reduce Poverty to Accelerate Sustainable Development January 31.10.2000. World Bank.

I.G. Patel – 1998
Economic Reform and Global Change. Macmillan India Ltd., Delhi.

I.J.Ahulwalia & IMD Little – 1998
India Economic Reforms and Development. Oxford University Press.

Asian Development Bank – 1994.
Rural Poverty in Developing Asia. ADB Manila.

A.M. Khusro – 1999
The Poverty of Nations. Macmillan Press Ltd., London.

Institute of Applied Man-Power Research – 1996
Poverty and Employment. New Age International Publisher, Delhi.

Rajah J. Chellaih & R. Sudarshan (Ed) – 1999
Income –Poverty and beyond. Social Science Press, New Delhi.

Uma Kapila (Ed.) 1999
Indian Economy since Independence. Academic Foundations.

C. Steven Larue (Ed.) – 1997
The India Handbook. Fitzroy Dear Boll Publishers.

S.P. Gupta – 1998
Post Reform India : Emerging Trends. Allied Publishers, New Delhi.

Jean Dreze and A. Sen – 1995
Economic Development and social opportunity.
Oxford University Press, New Delhi.

Government of India
Five-year Plans, New Delhi. (Fourth to Ninth Five Year Plan.)
Planning Commission.

M. Lipton –1997
Urban Bias in World Development. London, Templeton.

Government of India – 1997
Economic Survey 1996-1997, 1998, 1999, 2000.
Economic Division, Ministry of Finance, New Delhi.

Government of India –1993
Report of the Expert Group on Estimation of Proportion and Number of Poor, Perspective Planning Division.
Planning Commission, New Delhi

Waging the Global War on Poverty Wide Article entitled Public, Private. Social Development and Poverty Revolution. The Kerala Model by M. H. SURYA NARAYAN.

United Nations
Growth with Equity : Policy, Lessons from the experience of selected Asian countries. Article entitled Growth with Equity. Policy lessons from the Experience of India by Manoj Panda.

Spectrum
The Magazine of SAARC Secretariat, Nov. 1996 – Poverty Eradication – A major challenge to SAARC; SAARC Secretariat, Kathmandu.

Economic and Political weekly, Jan 6, 2001 Article entitled – Non Conventional Indicators : Gender, Disparities under structural reforms By Shobna Sonpar, Ravi Kapur

Economic and Political Weekly – July 15 – 21, 2000 – Article entitled – Theme Distribution Expenditure Pattern and Social indicators By B.K. Pradhan, P.K. Roy, M.R. Saluja, Shanta Venkatam.

Economic and Political Weekly – July 18 – 24 1998 Article entitled – Economic Reforms and the Poor emerging scenario By V.N. Rao

Economic and Political Weekly – March 4 – 10, 2000 – Article entitled – Economic Reforms, Poverty Income Distribution and Employment By S.M. Dev.

Economic and Political Weekly – March 25 – 31, 2000 – Article entitled – "What is needed for a more Pro-Poor Growth Process in India By Martin Ravallian.

M.G. Quebria (Ed) – 1994
Poverty in Developing Asia. Asian Development Bank, Manila.

Asian Development Outlook – 1997, 1998, 1999, 2000.
ADB, Manila

National Council of
Applied Economic Research, Indian Human Development Report – Oxford- 1999.

CHAPTER V

Felix Moses Edoho (Ed) – 1997
Globalisation and the New World order, Praeger Publishers Westport.

James H. Mittelman (Ed) – 1997
Globalisation : Critical Reflections, Lynne Rienner Publishers, London

Jonathan Mischie, John Gieve Smith (Ed) – 1998
Globalisation, Growth and Governance, Oxford University Press New York

Charles E. Morrison, Hadi Soesastro (Ed) – 1998
Domestic Adjustments to Globalisation, Japan center for international Exchange Tokyo, New York.

Dean Baker, Gerald Epstein, Rolurt Pollin (Ed) – 1998
Globalisation and Progressive Economic Policy, Cambridge University Press

Peter Dicken – 1998
Global Shift : Transforming The World Economy, The Guilford Press : New York

Horst Siebert – 1999
The World Economy, Routledge London

The World Bank – 1999
Annual World Conference on Development Economics, The World Bank

D. Achi Kgi (Ed) – 1999
Innovatioin Policy in a Global Economy, Cambridge University Press

John H. Dunning, Khabil A. Hamdani – 1997
The New Globalism and Developing Countries, UN University Press

Richard Layard – 1999
Tackling Inequality, Macmillan Press Ltd. London.

OECD
Participatory Development, OECD Paris.

Deepa Narayan – 2000
Voices of the Poor : Can Anyone hear?, Oxford University Press

The World Bank – 1998 to 2000
World Development Report, Oxford University Press.

The World Bank – 1998 to 2000
Global Economic Prospects and Developing Countries, World Bank

United Nations – 1998 to 2000
World Economic and Social Survey, United Nations

UNDP – 1997 to 2000
Human Development Report (1997-2000), Oxford University Press

UNCTAD – 1998 to 2000
Trade and Development Report, UNCTAD

Nagire Woods (Ed) – 2000
The Political economy of Globalisation, Macmillan Press Ltd. London

Richard E. Mashomba – 2000
Africa in the Global Economy, Lynne Rienner Publishers : Boulder, London

Vincent Cavle – 1999
Globalisation and Global governance , The Royal Institute of International Affaires

UNDP – 1998
Overcoming Human Poverty – UNDP Poverty Report 1998, UNDP

Aseem Prakash and Jeffrey A. Hart (Ed) – 1999
Responding to Globalisation, Routledge, New York

UNCTAD – 1996
Globalisation and Liberalisation – Effects of International Economic Relations on Poverty, UNCTAD

Vinod Ahuja, Benu Bidani, Francisco Ferira, Michael Walton – 1997
Everyone's Miracle-Revisit Poverty and Inequality in East Asia, The World Bank

The World Bank – 1993
The East Asian Miracle, The World Bank

UNCTAD – 2000
10th Session of UNCTAD (19th February 2000), UNCTAD

UNDP – 2000
Overcoming Human Poverty, UNDP

ILO – 1996
International Labour Review, ILO Geneva

United Nations – 2000
Report of the Secretary General – 54th Session- Agenda item 49 B-The Millennium Assembly of the United Nations, United Nations.

UNCTAD – 1999
Report of the Secretary General UNCTAD to UNCTAD X – Tenth Session Bangkok, Thailand 12-19 February 2000, UNCTAD

Vito Tanzi, Ke-Young Chu, Sanjeev Gupta – 1999
Economic Policy and Equity, International Monetary Fund

United Nations –2000
United Nations Millennium Declaration, United Nations.

International Monetary Fund – 1997 to 2000, World Economic Outlook (1997 to 2000), IMF

Jean Dreze and Amaritya Sen and Athar Hussain (Ed) and Amartya Sen and Athar Hussain (Ed)
The Political Economy of Hunger, Oxford University Press

ESCAP – 1999
ESCAP Report for 1999. ESCAP

Santosh Mehrotra, Richard Jolly – 1997
Development with a Human Face, Clarendon Press Oxford

Ulrich Hiemenz (Ed) – 1999
Growth and Competition in the New Global Economy, OECD 1999

C. Col. Clough, James Manor – 1991
State of Market, Clarendon Press Oxford.

B. Ramesh Babu (Ed) – 1998
Globalization and the South Asian State,
South Asian Publisher Pvt. Ltd. New Delhi.

Kamala Sinha (Ed) – 1999
Globalization and Developing Countries, New Age International Publishers.

Mitsuhiro Kagami, John Humphiey Michael Piore
Learning, Liberalization and Economic Adjustment, Institute of Developing, Economies, Tokyo.

John-Ren Chen (Ed)
Economic Effects of Globalization, Ashgate Publishing Limited, House, Croft Road, Aldershot, Hampshire GU11 3HR England

Assaf Razin, Efraim Sadka – 1999
Economics of Globalization – Policy perspectives from Public Economics, Cambridge University Press 1999 – New York.

Deepak Lal and H. Myint – 1996
The Political Economy of Poverty, Equity, and Growth
Clarendon Press, Oxford.

Michael Lipton – 1997
Why Poor People Stay Poor – Urban Bias in World Development
Temple Smith ,London

Yujiro Hayami – 1997
Development Economics, Clarendon Press – Oxford

Michel Beaud, Gilles Dostaler
Economic Thought since Keynes, Routledge – London and New York

Centre for International Relations Faculty for Social Sciences University of Ljubljano – 1996

Development and International Cooperation – Volume XII Number 22-June 1996 Center for International Relations Faculty for Social Sciences University of Ljubljano.

Paul Streeten with Shahid Javed, Burki Mahbub Ul Haq., Norman Hicks Stewart Frances – 1998

First Things First ; Meeting Basic Human Needs in the Developing Countries, Published for the World Bank Oxford University Press

John Cameroun with Hans Ranbark and Ken Cole – 1995

Poverty and Power, Oxford University Press – Delhi/Bombay, Calcutta, Madras

Food and Agriculture Organisation of United Nations Regional Office for Asia and the Pacific December 1998 – 1999
Poverty and Food Security in Asia, RAP Publication.

Malcolm Gillis, Dwight H. Perkins, Michael Roemer, Donald R. Snodgrass – 1996

Economics of Development, W.W., Norton & Company – New York London

P.R. Bhrahmananda
Amartya Sen and Welfare Economics, Sudha Publications No. 1, Annadanappa Lane, Avenue Road Cross, Bangalore – 560002

Theodore W. Schultz – 1993
The Economics of Being Poor, Blackwell

Bon Ho Koo, Dwight H. Perkins – 1995
Social capability and Long Term Economic Growth, Macmillan Press Ltd.

Mitchell A. Seligson, John Passee-Smith – 1993
Development and Underdevelopment, Lyynee Reinner Publisher Boulder, Colarado – USA.

Malcolm Ruther Ford – 1994
Institutions in Economics, Cambridge University Press

S. Ghatak – 1995
Introduction to Development Economics

Shahid Yusuf, Weiping Wu, Simon Evenett – 2000
Local Dynamics in an Era of Globalisation, Oxford University Press

Raundi Hal Vorson, Quevedo Hartmut Schneider – 2000
Waging The Global War on Poverty, Development Assistance Committee (EECD).

Martin Godfrey – 1996
Global Unemployment : The New Challenge to Economic Theory, Wheatsheaf Books Ltd.

Phillipe Aghion and Jeffrey G. Williams on – 1998
Growth, Inequality and Globalization : Theory, History and Policy, Cambridge University Press.

Horst Siebert – 1999
The World Economy, Routledge – London New York

H.W. Arndt, Hal Hill – 1999
Southeast Asia's Economic Crisis, Institute of Southeast Asian Studies

James H. Mittelman – 1996
Globalisation : Critical Reflections, Lynne Rienner Publishers Boulder London

Jonathan Michie, Gohn Grieve Smith – 1998
Globalization and Technology, Oxford University Press New York

The World Bank Group – 2000
Prospects for Development, The World Bank

Jan Knippers Black – 1999
Development in theory and Practice : West View Press.

Index